Your Florida Guide to Perennials

Florida A&M University, Tallahassee

Florida Atlantic University, Boca Raton

Florida Gulf Coast University, Ft. Myers

Florida International University, Miami

Florida State University, Tallahassee

University of Central Florida, Orlando

University of Florida, Gainesville

University of North Florida, Jacksonville

University of South Florida, Tampa

University of West Florida, Pensacola

Your Florida Guide to
Perennials

Selection, Establishment, and Maintenance

 Sydney Park Brown
Rick K. Schoellhorn

FLORIDA EXTENSION SERVICE
Institute of Food and Agricultural Sciences
University of Florida

UNIVERSITY PRESS OF FLORIDA
Gainesville/Tallahassee/Tampa/Boca Raton
Pensacola/Orlando/Miami/Jacksonville/Ft. Myers

Copyright 2006 by Sydney Park Brown and Rick Schoellhorn

Printed in China on acid-free paper

All rights reserved

11 10 09 08 07 06   6 5 4 3 2 1

A record of cataloging-in-publication data is available
from the Library of Congress.

ISBN 0-8130-2927-9

The University Press of Florida is the scholarly publishing
agency for the State University System of Florida, comprising
Florida A&M University, Florida Atlantic University, Florida
Gulf Coast University, Florida International University, Florida
State University, University of Central Florida, University of
Florida, University of North Florida, University of South
Florida, and University of West Florida.

University Press of Florida
15 Northwest 15th Street
Gainesville, FL 32611-2079
http://www.upf.com

Contents

Acknowledgments

The authors gratefully acknowledge the contributions of Loretta Hodyss and David Marshall for their work on the IFAS/Extension publication *Flowering Perennials for Florida*, which was the foundation of this work. We would also like to express our appreciation to Rick Brown, Riverview Flower Farm, for his help in cultural information and photography.

We emphasize that survival and performance of perennials is highly variable, and for this reason, we have tried to err on the side of caution in our remarks. We encourage readers to share information with us so that we can refine this book in the future. Please contact us on the Web at *http://hort.ifas.ufl.edu*

*Combine annuals and perennials
for dramatic displays of color.*

one

Introduction to Perennials in Florida 🌿

Perennials come in a wonderful variety of forms and colors. There are perennials for every season in the Florida garden, so year-round color and interest are easy to achieve. Perennials can provide weeks, if not months, of flower color and even longer periods of attractive foliage. While annual flowers provide brief periods of brilliant color and high impact, the diverse hues and textures of perennial plants offer a more subtle air of change. When planning your Florida garden, think of annuals as the temporary stars of the landscape and the perennial plants as the loyal supporting cast.

Here in Florida, where winters are mild, some perennials that are herbaceous in other parts of the country become woody shrubs or small trees. Even within the state some plants behave as herbaceous perennials in North Florida and woody perennials in South Florida.

Also keep in mind that plants that behave as perennials in some areas of the United States may not be reliable in the deep south because they require cool nights, long, cold winters, and/or low humidity to survive from year to year. These plants suffer during Florida's hot, humid summers and should be used like cool season annuals. For similar reasons, Mediterranean plants that thrive as perennials in drier climates are also best used like cool season annuals. Such plants usually stop flowering and succumb to disease with the onset of Florida's summer rains and heat.

For best results in the Florida garden, rely on tropical perennials that thrive in temperatures of 55–95°F. They perform year-round in South Florida where winters are mild. Tropical perennials may be damaged by frosts or freezes in central and north Florida and may even die to the ground, but they quickly recover from their roots in

Perennials like Firespike have a long bloom season and attractive glossy green foliage the rest of the year.

Heat and humidity–loving tropical perennials like Pentas thrive in Florida landscapes.

spring. Extremely cold winters may kill a tropical perennial entirely. A good example of a tropical perennial is Pentas (*Pentas lanceolata*). It becomes a small woody shrub in South Florida, but dies back each winter in North Florida. Other examples include Jacobinia (*Justicia carnea*), Ornamental Sweet Potato (*Ipomoea batatas*), and *Crossandra*.

Does all of this sound confusing or difficult? Relax. Gardening with perennials is really very easy and rewarding. Use this book as a reference, consult your local county extension agent, talk with other gardeners and local garden experts, and visit Florida's many botanic and display gardens. You'll discover a huge selection of plants that offer lavish colors, tropical tones, and phenomenal results for Florida gardeners.

Examples of Plants Best Treated as Cool-Season Annuals in Florida:

Marguerite Daisy (*Argyranthemum* hybrids)
African Daisy (*Osteospermum* hybrids)
Anemone
Bearded Iris
Brachyscome
Delphinium
Fuchsia
Geranium
Gazania

Gazania—a perennial in other parts of the country—often performs best as a cool season annual in Florida.

Display gardens like this one at EPCOT are a great source of ideas for home landscapes.

Perennials Redefined

The textbook definition of a perennial plant is "a plant that grows indefinitely, remaining or returning on its own roots each year." An annual, by contrast, is a plant that grows, flowers, re-seeds, and dies usually within a single growing season. The perennials that perform well in Florida and are included here are, for the most part, herbaceous perennials—plants that have soft or succulent tissue with little or no woody tissue. They may be evergreen or lose their foliage in the winter, but the roots survive and the foliage returns in spring.

In summary, remember these guidelines when selecting and growing perennials in Florida:

1 Florida's climate varies dramatically from north to south and makes "perennial" a relative term. Perennials that thrive in Miami may not be hardy in North Florida and North Florida perennials may not survive in Miami. {Sidebar 1.02 near here}

2 Perennial does not mean "immortal." It is a misconception to assume that a perennial will live forever. Some need to be re-planted or rejuvenated every three to five years.

3 Experiment and have fun. Remember, every garden is a "work in progress."

Philippine Violet is a good example of a tropical perennial that can perform in sun or part shade.

two

Getting Started

Bed Location, Design, and Preparation

Perennials can be mixed in with shrubs and trees, grown in containers, or used in flower beds. When designing a new bed, consider how you can maximize the aesthetics and enjoyment of your future garden and minimize your workload. Bed preparation and upkeep can be laborious and time consuming, so make sure your plans are realistic.

Before designing a perennial bed or planting a single plant, consider the following:

Exposure/Sunlight

Sunlight will determine which plants you'll choose for your garden. Most perennials require at least four hours of direct sun to perform their best. However, some prefer a shady setting and will not tolerate much sun. Remember, surrounding shrubs and trees will compete for root space, moisture, and nutrients. As a result, these areas may demand more water and fertilizer.

Keep in mind that in summer, the path of the sun is directly overhead, whereas in winter, the sun's path is in the southern sky. The intense sunlight and high temperatures of summer can take their toll, and some perennials may perform better in the summer if shaded during part of the day.

Use perennials in containers as well as in the garden.

Nothing tolerates a full day of hot sun better than Lantana 'Gold Mound.'

Use a hose to easily lay out the shape of a perennial bed.

Size, Shape, and Views

Use a garden hose to outline the borders of your proposed bed. This allows you to easily adjust its shape and size before you start digging. Look at the bed from different areas of your yard. What existing plants or structures will enhance or hide it? Also, consider views from inside the home through windows, glass doors, or porches.

Borders

What will surround your plant bed? Ground cover? lawn? mulch? or "hard-scape" such as a brick border, a deck, or a patio? If your flower bed will be bordered by lawn, visualize how you will mow around it. Actually negotiate the curves and angles of the bed with your mower and adjust your borders where it is difficult or cumbersome to steer it.

Bed Preparation

The single most important thing you can do for a Florida garden is to improve the soil. Unless otherwise indicated, the plants listed in the Perennial Selection Guide in chapter 3 grow and bloom best in moist but well-drained soils that have been amended with organic matter. A well-prepared bed will save you future headaches and allow your garden to reach its full potential.

Once you have determined the outline of your bed, you may want to use an herbicide to kill existing weeds or grass.

The first step is to remove any existing weeds, grass, or other plants that won't be incorporated into the design. Grass and weeds can be removed by hand or with a sod cutter, or you can apply a nonselective herbicide such as glyphosate. Spray unwanted plants, being careful that the herbicide does not drift onto nearby lawn and landscape plants. You can also smother and kill existing grass and weeds with heavy layers of newspaper, carpet, or black plastic. It is best to remove the dead vegetation as it may harbor pests. However, this is not absolutely necessary because it will eventually decay and mix into the soil.

Add at least six inches of organic matter such as compost, potting soil, leaf mold, or manure to new beds. This will increase the soil's ability to

Weeds or grass can also be removed by hand.

hold moisture and nutrients and enhance the performance of most perennials. A shovel can be used to mix in the amendments, but for large beds a tiller will save time and muscles. Till or dig the bed to a depth of at least six inches. This provides a zone of rich, loose soil in which roots can quickly establish. Continue to add organic matter each time you replant an area. South Florida gardeners may encounter soils high in limestone and marl that are difficult to cultivate. In this case, add organic matter (as much as several feet) on top of the ground.

Most perennials prefer an acid soil, with pH between 5.5 and 7.0. Your county Extension office can provide information on soil types in your area and how and where to have your soil pH tested. Add fertilizer before you till or dig, as well as a soil acidifier or neutralizer if suggested by your soil pH test. Experts recommend that Florida gardeners use controlled-release fertilizers or organic fertilizers such as bone meal or blood meal. Products such as these will provide nutrients all season.

"Beef-up" Your Soil with Organic Matter

Examples of organic matter are peat moss, manure, leaf mold, and compost. Compost is dark brown in color, but still has both large and small chunks of bark, leaves, and other plant materials visible in the blend. Organic matter acts as a slow-release plant food as it decomposes. Materials that are not well-composted will rob nitrogen from the soil and can have toxic effects on roots. It is best to use "unfinished" compost as mulch (or top dressing), not as a soil amendment.

Organic materials should be added to the entire bed to help retain water and nutrients.

Contact your local county Extension office for information on soil testing.

Slow-release fertilizers are recommended for Florida.

Fertilizer Types

There are four basic types of fertilizer: organic materials like compost or manures, granular fertilizers, soluble fertilizers that are dissolved in water, and controlled-release products such as Osmocote, Nutricote, Dynamite, and others. Controlled-release fertilizers are more costly but the nutrients in them are slowly and steadily delivered to the plants over an extended period of several months. Perennials benefit from this small but constant supply of nutrients and this type of fertilizer is less likely to leach or run off.

Perennial beds should be tilled or dug several weeks before planting.

After digging and amending the soil, level and smooth the bed.

Once your bed is amended, leveled, and smoothed, it is ready for planting. Some gardeners prefer to let the soil settle for three to seven days so that new plants don't sink into the loose soil and end up too deeply planted. It is also easier to mulch once the soil has settled. Now the real fun of selecting and planting perennials begins!

Masses of Gerbera Daisies brighten a part shade area.

The Right Perennial in the Right Place

3.1. How to Garden with Perennials

This chapter will help familiarize you with many perennials and the role they can play in your garden. Unlike annuals, which are best used in the forefront of beds to maximize their impact, perennials usually form the secondary component of a plant bed.

When designing a bed, consider plant form and texture. Pleasing foliage combinations (e.g., clumping forms with upright forms; delicate textures combined with bold) give the garden interest long after the flowers are gone. Use perennials with attractive or colorful leaves as centerpieces or accent plants because they provide year-round appeal.

The role that a perennial plays in a garden is largely determined by four factors: season of flower, nonflowering appearance, growth habit, and color.

Season of Flower

Many perennials bloom year-round while others have distinct flowering seasons. This information is included in the Perennial Selection Guide in this chapter and will help you plan attractive displays and plant combinations. Most perennials put on their best display in spring, early summer, and fall. Summer heat and humidity prevent all but tropical perennials from performing their best.

The bold leaves of Elephant Ear provide a tropical flair, and the contrasting foliage of the Coleus provides season-long interest.

It is important to think about when you enjoy gardening and when you spend the most time in your yard. For example, gardeners in southern and central Florida will want to include perennials that bloom during the mild and enjoyable winter season. Fall and spring are more important in North Florida where the harsh winters kill back many perennials.

Ideally, a garden should have a succession of spring, summer, and fall/winter performers. Think of the different views of your garden and try to include seasonal color in each view. This approach takes planning and familiarity with each perennial you plant. Most gardeners learn by experimenting and mistakes and luckily even "mistakes" are often beautiful.

Agapanthus and *Verbena* perform best in late spring to early summer and should be mixed with perennials that provide interest in other seasons.

Nonflowering Appearance

Some perennials remain attractive most of the year. Others go dormant or become less appealing in their off season. To maximize year-round color, intersperse different types of perennials so they camouflage each other as they alternately flourish and fade.

Growth Habit

Perennials that grow in northern states rarely attain large sizes because of winter dieback and a shorter growing season. This is not the case in Florida. In the southern portion of the state, many tropical perennials grow rapidly to large sizes and are seldom damaged by cold. So size becomes a major consideration in planning a garden.

Because it can grow very large Flowering Maple is best suited to the back of the flower border.

Traditionally, taller plants are placed at the back of the flower bed where they will not block the view or overwhelm shorter companion plants. In small gardens, larger plants may not be desired. However, for a truly tropical look, the bold texture of large perennial plants can't be beat. Check the maximum plant sizes listed in the Perennial Selection Guide and remember that frequent pruning may be required to keep taller perennials from growing too large.

In general, small to medium-sized perennials are used to best advantage when they are planted in masses. The bold displays of color they provide are generally more pleasing than individual plants placed here and there. Evergreen or flowering shrubs provide a nice backdrop for large drifts of perennials or they can be mixed into a perennial bed to provide protection, support, or a screen for perennials not in flower.

The growth habits of some perennials change when they flower. For example, coneflower (*Echinacea*), *Gerbera*, and daylily (*Hemerocallis*) produce flowers on lofty spikes above the foliage. Place them where their tall flowers won't obscure smaller plants.

Society Garlic makes a beautiful mass display.

The plant form of Daylily changes when it begins to flower.

Color

Flower and foliage color is another important design consideration. "Hot" colors such as orange, red, and yellow stand out in the garden. "Cool" colors, such as blues, purples, and pinks provide a more restful atmosphere, but don't show up as well in the landscape. These different color groups can be massed for a dramatic effect or mixed for a less formal garden. White, silver/gray, green, and purple/black foliage and flowers work with all other colors and can be used as transition plants in the garden.

The color wheel is a useful tool for mixing colors in the garden. There are three basic approaches for combining colors. A *monochromatic* color scheme uses lighter and darker values of one color. An example would be a white garden where all the flowers and foliage are white or off-white. *Analogous* color schemes combine colors that are next to each other on the color wheel. An analogous color scheme could include red, red-violet, violet-red, violet, and purple. A *complementary* color scheme combines colors directly opposite on the color wheel. For example, a combination of orange Crossandra and blue Torenia is a complementary color scheme. Perennials are listed by color in Perennials for Special Uses and Conditions at the end of this chapter.

The silver tones of Wormwood and Ornamental Sweet Potato make them good transition plants in the landscape.

This planting is an example of an analogous color scheme.

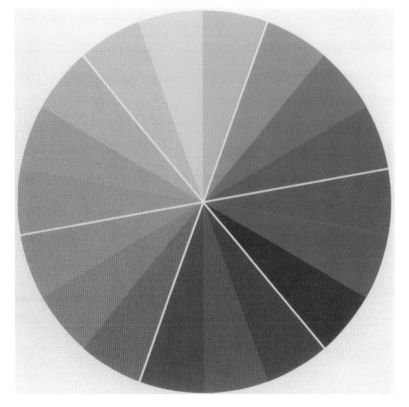

The color wheel can help you combine flower colors.

Pointers to Remember

The perennials listed and described on the following pages are good performers in Florida. As you select perennials for your garden, use these pointers to help you achieve greater success:

1 Use evergreen and flowering shrubs as the backdrop for your garden. These shrubs will provide permanent "walls" against which your perennial flowers can come and go with the changing seasons. Examples include *Gardenia, Camellia, Brunfelsia, Thryallis*, and many others.

2 Note the mature size and flowering season of each perennial you select. Remember, the growth habit of certain perennials changes dramatically when they flower.

3 How much sunlight does the plant require? No amount of water, fertilizer, or care will make a perennial bloom if it does not receive the amount of light it needs.

4 How cold tolerant is it? Does the foliage die back naturally in winter or when frosts or freezes occur? If so, place it where it will not be missed in winter.

5 Consider plant form and texture. Pleasing foliage combinations (i.e., rounded forms with upright forms; delicate textures with bold leaves) give the garden interest long after flowers fade.

6 "Hot" colors such as orange, red, and yellow should be grouped together and segregated from "cool" hues and pastels such as blue, purple, and pink. White, silver, and green go with everything and can be used as transition colors in the garden.

Evergreen and flowering shrubs form the backdrop to perennials in this garden.

The combination of foliage colors and textures is appealing even without flowers.

3.2. Perennial Selection Guide

This section will help you select perennials for your landscape. The plants are arranged in alphabetical order by scientific name. Common names are listed in the index. Refer to the hardiness-zone map below to determine if a plant is suitable for your region of the state. Please note: The cultural information listed for each plant represents the *optimal* conditions; some perennials will perform satisfactorily with less than ideal conditions. The section titled Plants for Special Uses and Conditions provides lists of plants by color, form, use, etc. Some terms used in the selection guide may be unfamiliar; this short glossary defines the terms used.

The state can be divided into hardiness zones indicated by numbers on this map. Each zone is divided into A (the cooler part of the zone) and B (the warmer part of the zone).

LIGHT

Full Sun: plant requires full sun all or most of the day to grow and/or flower properly.

Full sun to part shade: plant grows equally well in full sun, filtered shade, or part shade (fewer than four hours of full sun a day).

Part to full shade: requires protection from full sun; needs shade.

SALT TOLERANCE

Moderate salt tolerance: can be grown on the protected side of an oceanfront building; is often injured by salt-laden winds during a storm.

High salt tolerance: can tolerate conditions on an ocean or gulf side of a beachfront building.

COLD TOLERANCE

Hardy: frost and freeze hardy.

Semi-hardy: some plant damage from frost or freeze.

Tender: plant is killed to the ground by freezing temperatures, but recovers from roots.

Upright: a plant form that is more vertical than horizontal.

Rounded: a plant form that is curved or globe shaped.

Ground cover: a low-growing plant that is more horizontal than vertical.

USES

Massing: a method of planting where perennials of the same species are grouped together to create a visual mass effect.

Accent plant: a single plant, usually with bold or dramatic foliage or color that is used to catch the eye.

Back of border: large perennials that should be placed toward the back of a perennial border or plant bed.

Mid-border: mid-sized perennials that should be positioned toward the center of a perennial border or plant bed.

Front of border: small or low-growing perennials best used in the very front of a perennial border or plant bed.

Attracts butterflies/hummingbirds: a nectar-rich perennial that is a food source for butterflies and/or hummingbirds.

Container plant: a plant that is particularly appealing or dramatic when planted in a decorative pot.

OTHER

Drought tolerant: a plant that, once established, may require irrigation only during prolonged periods without rainfall.

Native plant: a plant considered indigenous to Florida.

Invasive: a non-native plant that may spread by seed or underground stems into a landscape or natural area.

Aggressive: a plant which grows so rampantly it may crowd out other plants in the garden.

Deadheading: a pruning technique where old blooms and seed heads are removed for aesthetic reasons and to encourage new flowers.

Bract: A modified, sometimes showy, leaf associated with a flower.

Latin name: *Abutilon hybridum*

Common name: Flowering Maple

Hardiness zones: 8b–10

Plant form/height: mounding to upright/variable by type

Florida native: no (South America)

Cold tolerance: tender

Flower color/season: many colors and bi-colors/spring, fall

Leaf color/texture: medium green and variegated/ coarse

Light: full sun to part shade

Soil: rich, organic for best flowering

Salt tolerance: medium

Pest problems: spider mites

Uses: mid-border to back of border, container, hanging basket; attracts butterflies/hummingbirds

Method of propagation: cuttings

Narrative: Many cultivars and species. See Hibiscus: Bold and Colorful (page 57–59) for more information on this and other members of the Hibiscus group.

Latin name: *Achillea* species

Common name: Yarrow

Hardiness zones: 8a–9a

Plant form/height: rounded, spreading ground cover/ 6–12 inches; flowers to 18–36 inches

Florida native: no (temperate Northern Hemisphere)

Cold tolerance: hardy

Flower color/season: pink, yellow, white/spring

Leaf color/texture: light green/fine

Light: sun

Soil: well drained, very drought tolerant, wide pH range

Salt tolerance: low

Pest problems: generally pest free

Uses: massing, cut flower, ground cover, front of border

Method of propagation: division, seed

Narrative: Most of the 60–100 species have attractive feathery or ferny foliage. Often declines during periods of hot, rainy weather. May require staking. Good cut or dried flower. Popular species include *A. millefolium* and *A. taygetea*.

Latin name: *Agapanthus* species

Common name: Lily of the Nile

Hardiness zones: 8a–11

Plant form/height: rounded, clumping/2 feet; flowers to 3 feet

Florida native: no (South Africa)

Cold tolerance: semi-hardy

Flower color/season: blue, lavender, or white/summer, early fall

Leaf color/texture: medium green/coarse

Light: sun to part shade

Soil: fertile, well drained

Salt tolerance: medium

Pest problems: grasshoppers, slugs

Uses: massing, mid-border, cut flower

Method of propagation: seed, division

Narrative: The evergreen, strap-shaped leaves are handsome year-round. Dwarf and variegated forms are available. Needs winter protection in North Florida (zones 8a and 8b); is short lived in South Florida (zones 10–11).

Latin name: *Allamanda cathartica* 'Schottii'

Common name: Bush Allamanda

Hardiness zones: 9b–11

Plant form/height: rounded/2–4 feet

Florida native: no (Brazil)

Cold tolerance: semi-hardy

Flower color/season: yellow/year-round

Leaf color/texture: bright green/medium

Light: sun to part shade

Soil: moist but well drained, somewhat drought tolerant

Salt tolerance: medium

Pest problems: whitefly; generally pest free

Uses: accent plant, massing, mid-border, container

Method of propagation: cuttings, seed

Narrative: The sap of *Allamanda* is poisonous. Remove fruit pods to stimulate blooming. *A. blanchetii* (also sold as *A. violacea*) has purple flowers. *Mandevilla*, a close relative, is a vine with beautiful pink flowers. The genus *Urchites*, often sold as *Allamanda*, has glossy leaves and yellow trumpet-shaped flowers.

Latin name: *Alocasia, Colocasia, Xanthosoma*

Common names: Elephant Ear, Taro
Hardiness zones: 8a–11
Plant form/height: upright, some types spread/variable by type
Florida native: no
Cold tolerance: tender
Flower color/season: flowers are not showy
Leaf color/texture: variable by type/coarse
Light: sun to shade depending on type
Soil: good garden soil to boggy conditions
Salt tolerance: low
Pest problems: few
Uses: back of border, accent plant, container, water gardens
Method of propagation: tubers, division
Narrative: See Elephant Ears are Tropical, Easy, and Rewarding (pages 44–45) for more information.

Latin name: *Alternanthera* species

Common names: Joseph's Coat, Parrot Leaf, Calico Plant
Hardiness zones: 9b–11
Plant form/height: upright, rounded, or ground cover/ variable by type
Florida native: no
Cold tolerance: semi-hardy
Flower color/season: flowers not showy/seasonal leaf color
Leaf color/texture: variegated or purple/fine to medium
Light: sun to part shade
Soil: moist, rich
Salt tolerance: medium
Pest problems: diseases and chewing insects on dwarf forms
Uses: foliage interest primarily; front of border; formally clipped into shapes
Method of propagation: cuttings
Narrative: Many cultivars of *A. ficoidea* exist with white, yellow, pink, red and/or bronze variegations. Leaf colors intensify during cool months. *A. dentata* 'Purple Knight' reaches 36 inches and is upright with dark purple leaves. *Alternanthera* is often confused with *Iresine*, a related group of plants.

Latin name: *Angelonia angustifolia*

Common name: Angelonia

Hardiness zones: 9a–10

Plant form/height: upright/2–3 feet,

Florida native: no (Mexico, West Indies)

Cold tolerance: semi-hardy

Flower color/season: violet, pink, blue, white, blue/white striped/year-round

Leaf color/texture: dark green/fine

Light: sun

Soil: fertile, moist

Salt tolerance: low

Pest problems: generally pest free

Uses: massing, mid-border

Method of propagation: cuttings

Narrative: The lance-shaped, pointed leaves of *Angelonia* contrast nicely with other plants. Flowers are fragrant.

Latin name: *Artemisia* species

Common name: Wormwood

Hardiness zones: 8a–9b

Plant form/height: rounded/variable by type

Florida native: no (Siberia, Europe)

Cold tolerance: hardy

Flower color/season: flowers not showy

Leaf color/texture: gray to silver/fine

Light: sun

Soil: dry, not tolerant of wet conditions

Salt tolerance: medium

Pest problems: generally pest free

Uses: mid-border, transition plant, Mediterranean effect

Method of propagation: cuttings

Narrative: Needs good drainage and air circulation. Do not crowd in flower beds. *A.* x 'Powis Castle' and *A. ludoviciana* 'Silver King' are reliable gray forms; 'Oriental Limelight' (*A. vulgaris*) has yellow and green variegated foliage. Heat and humidity limit the use of many types. Fragrant foliage.

Latin name: *Asclepias* species

Common name: Milkweed

Hardiness zones: 8a–11 (depending on species)

Plant form/height: upright/variable by type

Florida native: *A. perennis* and *A. tuberosa* among others; (*A. curassavica*—South America)

Cold tolerance: variable by species; see Narrative

Flower color/season: white, orange, red-orange, and yellow depending on species/year-round

Leaf color/texture: variable by type

Light: sun

Soil: moist for *A. perennis*; well drained for *A. curassavica*; very dry for *A. tuberosa*.

Salt tolerance: high for *A. tuberosa*

Pest problems: aphids, milkweed bugs

Uses: attracts butterflies/hummingbirds; *A. perennis* for water gardens.

Method of propagation: seed, cuttings

Narrative: *A. curassavica* (Tropical/Scarlet Milkweed) is best for Central and South Florida. It readily reseeds. *A. perennis* (White Milkweed) is suited to North and Central; *A. tuberosa* (Butterfly Weed) grows wild throughout the state.

Latin name: *Aster* species

Common name: Aster

Hardiness zones: 8a–9a

Plant form/height: rounded/6–18 inches

Florida native: no (central and eastern North America)

Cold tolerance: hardy

Flower color/season: blue/lavender/spring, summer, fall

Leaf color/texture: silver gray/medium

Light: sun

Soil: well drained, somewhat drought tolerant

Salt tolerance: low

Pest problems: generally pest free

Uses: front of border, cut flower; attracts butterflies

Method of propagation: division, cuttings

Narrative: *A. laevis* is a small-flowered aster that is not very showy but very reliable in North Florida. *A. carolinianus* (Climbing Aster), a Florida native, is found in wet areas throughout the state, but adapts to well-drained sites. Provide support for this sprawling plant and enjoy a splendid display of small pink to pale purple flowers in fall.

Latin name: *Barleria cristata*

Common name: Philippine Violet
Hardiness zones: 8b–11
Plant habit: upright/3–4 feet
Florida native: no (India, Myanmar)
Cold tolerance: tender
Flower color/season: lavender or white/fall in North and Central Florida; year-round in South Florida
Leaf color/texture: dark green/medium
Light: sun to part shade
Soil: well drained, somewhat drought tolerant
Salt tolerance: none
Pest problems: generally pest free
Uses: back of border, specimen, massing
Method of propagation: cuttings, seed
Narrative: Readily reseeds itself and can become weedy. Prune to the ground each spring to maintain a bushy plant. Also available: *B. repens* (salmon, 12 inches tall, flowers in summer; spreads rampantly), *B. micans* (yellow flowers fall through early summer, 3 feet tall).

Latin name: *Begonia* species

Common name: Hardy Begonia
Hardiness zones: 8b–11
Plant form/height: upright, rounded, or ground cover depending on type/variable
Florida native: no (tropical and subtropical regions)
Cold tolerance: tender
Flower color/season: white, pinks, reds/winter, spring, some year-round
Leaf color/texture: variable by type/medium to coarse
Light: part to full shade
Soil: moist and organic
Salt tolerance: none to low
Pest problems: generally pest free; nematodes affect some types
Uses: Hosta replacements in the shade garden; best in Central to South Florida
Method of propagation: division, stem or leaf cuttings (depending on type)
Narrative: There are many Begonias with Florida landscape potential. See Beautiful Begonias for the Landscape (pages 32–33) for examples and more cultural information.

Dragon Wing Begonia

Baby Wing Begonia

Angel-wing Begonia

Beautiful Begonias for the Landscape

Landscape begonias are easy-to-grow tropical perennials that prefer warm temperatures, humidity, and moist, well-drained soil. They will rot if planted in a wet site or overwatered. Several hours of morning sun is the ideal light condition, although many begonias can tolerate more sunlight if kept moist. Fertilize them several times a year with a controlled-release fertilizer. Landscape begonias generally fall into three groups: Wax Begonias, Cane or Angel-wing Begonias, and rhizomatous begonias. Tuberous and Rieger begonias, two additional groups, do not usually make reliable landscape plants in Florida. Rieger begonias perform best as containerized plants; tuberous begonias are short-lived florist plants.

Wax Begonias (*Begonia semperflorens*) are normally considered annuals although they can often survive in the landscape for several years. There are numerous single- and double-flowered hybrids, and in general this group is popular and reliable. Consider visiting one of the state's Begonia Society meetings to see what a fantastic array of begonias you can grow in Florida.

Cane or Angel-wing Begonias have upright stems and clusters of dangling flowers in shades of red, orange, pink, or white. Flowers are produced year-round. The winglike leaves are sometimes spotted, banded, or splotched with color. Landscape favorites include 'Mary Elizabeth Moultrie' (pink flowers), 'Torch' (red flowers), and 'Alba' (ever-blooming white). 'Sophie Cecile' is a reluctant bloomer, but its robust, five-foot foliage makes it a landscape standout. For South Florida gardeners these plants provide year-round interest. In North Florida they usually die to the ground in the winter.

Water Lily Begonia with ferns.

Rhizomatous Begonias in the landscape

A collection of rhizomatous begonias: Star Begonia, Water Lily Begonia and 'Passing Storm' Begonia.

Begonia popenoei

Rhizomatous begonias have thick rhizomes that either grow somewhat upright or run along the ground. The flowers of the best landscape types are produced on stems above the foliage in winter and spring. North Florida gardeners get to see the fantastic blooms only if they plant in very protected areas or grow these plants in containers. Common types are the 'Star Begonia' (*Begonia heracleifolia*); hybrids such as 'Beefsteak' and 'Joe Hayden'; *B. nelumbifolia*, the "Water Lily Begonia"; and 'Passing Storm,' grown mostly for its beautiful lavender foliage. Many of these hybrids can have leaves up to two feet in diameter and make wonderful substitutes for Hostas in the landscape. The most colorful, the Rex Begonias, are also rhizomatous; because of foliage problems and a general preference for cooler climates these are often better houseplants than landscape plants. Still, try them for the boldest of foliage colors and a really unique shade garden.

Latin name: *Belamcanda chinensis*

Common names: Blackberry Lily, Leopard Lily

Hardiness zones: 8a–11

Plant form/height: upright, clumping/24 inches; flowers to 36 inches

Florida native: no (India, China, Japan, eastern former USSR)

Cold tolerance: hardy

Flower color/season: orange-red/summer, fall

Leaf color/texture: pale green/medium

Light: sun to part shade

Soil: well drained, very drought tolerant, wide pH range

Salt tolerance: unknown

Pest problems: crown rot disease if kept too wet; insect free

Uses: massing, accent plant, mid-border

Method of propagation: division, seed

Narrative: Blackberry lily has iris-like foliage and produces small, short-lived flowers that are light orange with red-orange spots. Numerous flowers are produced on long, branched stalks. Seed pods split to reveal clusters of black seeds, hence the common name Blackberry Lily; reseeds. 'Hello Yellow' is a shorter cultivar with pure yellow flowers.

Latin name: *Centratherum punctatum*

Common name: Brazilian Button Flower

Hardiness zones: 9a–11

Plant form/height: rounded/6–18 inches

Florida native: no (Brazil)

Cold tolerance: tender

Flower color/season: lavender/year-round

Leaf color/texture: dark green/coarse

Light: sun to part shade

Soil: well drained, very drought tolerant, wide pH range

Salt tolerance: unknown

Pest problems: generally pest free

Uses: massing, front of border; attracts butterflies

Method of propagation: cuttings, seed

Narrative: Bears long-lasting, fluffy flowers 1 inch across. Prune lightly to encourage denser foliage. Reseeds.

Latin name: *Cestrum* species

Common name: Tropical Jasmines

Hardiness zones: 8b–11

Plant form/height: rounded to upright/up to 15 feet depending on type

Florida native: no (tropical America)

Cold tolerance: hardy

Flower color/season: depends on species/fall, winter, spring

Leaf color/texture: medium green/medium

Light: sun, part shade

Soil: tolerant of a wide range of soils

Salt tolerance: low to moderate depending on type

Pest problems: mealybug, scale

Uses: back of the border, accent plant

Method of propagation: cuttings and seed

Narrative: All parts of *Cestrum* species are very poisonous. Night Blooming Jasmine (*Cestrum nocturnum*)—intensely fragrant flowers cause allergic reactions in some people; cold tender; moderately salt tolerant. Red Cestrum (*C. elegans*)—burgundy flowers, fall through spring, not fragrant; cold tender. Gold Cestrum (*C. aurantiacum*)—masses of golden yellow flowers on a shrub 6–15 feet tall, not fragrant; cold hardy; low salt tolerance.

Latin name: *Chrysanthemum grandiflora* (formerly *Dendranthema*)

Common names: Garden Chrysanthemum, Garden Mum

Hardiness zones: 8a–9b

Plant form/height: rounded, spreading/6–10 inches; flowers to 18–36 inches depending on type

Florida native: no (Asia)

Cold tolerance: hardy

Flower color/season: bronze, orange, red, white, yellow, pink, rose/fall, spring

Leaf color/texture: medium to dark green/medium

Light: sun to part shade

Soil: organic, acid, somewhat drought tolerant

Salt tolerance: medium

Pest problems: numerous

Uses: massing, cut flower; attracts butterflies

Method of propagation: division, cuttings

Narrative: Lightly prune from late spring through mid-August whenever plants grow to more than 6 inches by snipping off the top 2 inches of growth. After it blooms, prune off dead flower spikes. Some varieties produce tall flower spikes that must be staked. Good heirloom garden varieties exist only as "pass-along plants" (i.e., not available in the trade). For silver foliage, try *Ajania pacifica*.

Latin name: *Clerodendrum* species

Common name(s): many common names (see Narrative)
Hardiness zones: 8a–11
Plant form/height: upright shrubs, small trees or vines/ variable by height
Florida native: no (Africa, Asia)
Cold tolerance: variable by species; see Narrative
Flower color/season: many colors and forms/variable by type
Leaf color/texture: dark green or variegated/coarse
Light: sun to part shade
Soil: wide range, very drought tolerant
Salt tolerance: none to low depending on type
Pest problems: whitefly, spider mites, scale
Uses: depending on type: vine, shrub, small tree; attracts butterflies/hummingbirds
Method of propagation: cuttings, division, and seed
Narrative: See Clerodendrum: Good, Bad, and Ugly (pages 38–40).

Latin name: *Conoclinium coelestinum* (syn. *Eupatorium coelestinum*)

Common name: Mistflower
Hardiness zones: 8a–10b
Plant form/height: rounded, spreading/1–3 feet
Florida native: yes
Cold tolerance: tender
Flower color/season: blue or white/year-round
Leaf color/texture: medium green/medium
Light: sun to part shade
Soil: moist to wet
Salt tolerance: medium to high
Pest problems: generally pest free
Uses: wildflower gardens, water gardens
Method of propagation: cuttings, division, seed
Narrative: Provide room for its aggressive nature as it will spread by rhizomes and seed.

Latin name: *Crossandra infundibuliformis*

Common name: Crossandra
Hardiness zones: 9a–11
Plant form/height: rounded/1–4 feet
Florida native: no (India, Sri Lanka)
Cold tolerance: tender; foliage is injured by temperatures 40°F or below
Flower color/season: salmon, yellow, yellow-orange, red-orange/summer, fall
Leaf color/texture: light to medium green/medium
Light: sun to shade
Soil: well drained, acid, not drought tolerant
Salt tolerance: none to low
Pest problems: generally pest free
Uses: massing, mid- to back of border (depending on type)
Method of propagation: cuttings
Narrative: Not as sturdy the further north you go in the state, although it will occasionally reseed.

Latin name: *Cuphea hyssopifolia*

Common names: Mexican Heather, Hawaiian Heather
Hardiness zones: 8b–11
Plant form/height: rounded/1 foot
Florida native: no (Mexico)
Cold tolerance: tender
Flower color/season: purple, white/year-round
Leaf color/texture: medium green/fine
Light: sun to part shade
Soil: well drained, acid or alkaline
Salt tolerance: none to low
Pest problems: metallic beetles, root knot nematodes
Uses: massing, ground cover, front of border; attracts butterflies
Method of propagation: cutting
Narrative: Prune frequently but lightly to keep them compact and flowering. The cultivar 'Allyson' is more floriferous; 'Alba' has white flowers. Other Cupheas worth trying include Georgia Scarlet (*C. llavea*) —scarlet and purple blooms; Firefly Cuphea (*C. procumbens*)—large flowers from pink to scarlet and lavender; and Cigar Flower.

Flaming Glory Bower

Variegated Starburst Clerodendrum

Clerodendrum: Good, Bad, and Ugly

Some plants in the Clerodendrum group make wonderful landscape additions; others cause gardeners to weep and rue the day they ever planted one. Unfortunately, because plants in this latter group are so easy to grow and multiply so freely, they are frequently passed along from gardener to gardener without sufficient cautionary advice.

Before we look at the Clerodendrums you should avoid, let's look at those that are better behaved and, for the most part, as easy to grow as their troublesome cousins. Keep in mind, however, that many Clerodendrums tend to spread by underground stems and that they all need space.

Blue Butterfly Clerodendrum

Bleeding Heart Clerodendrum

Bleeding Heart Glory Bower (*Clerodendrum thomsoniae*) is a small vine excellent for partial shade in Central and South Florida. The attractive red flowers, which are surrounded by white calyces, appear during warm months of the year. Flaming Glory Bower (*C. splendens*) has masses of one-inch crimson flowers in winter. This vine or sprawling shrub needs support and is best grown in frostfree areas of Florida. Java Glory Bower (*C. speciosissimum*) is a large 3–5-foot shrub that will spread several feet. The brilliant scarlet flowers attract butterflies and hummingbirds. Butterflies also love the attractive blue flowers of *C. ugandense*. Blue Butterfly, as it is commonly called, can reach 12 feet in height. Blooms are produced in summer. It may reseed, but is easily controlled. Nodding Clerodendrum (*C. wallichii*, also known as *C. nutans*) is probably the classiest of the Clerodendrums with its

Nodding Clerodendrum (close up)

Nodding Clerodendrum

glossy, large green leaves and white butterfly-shaped blooms hanging downward in graceful, pretty arcs. Pagoda Flower (*C. paniculatum*) has showy, carmine pink to scarlet flower spikes that are uniquely tiered like an oriental pagoda. It can spread 3–5 feet, but is fairly easy to control. It grows throughout Florida but will die back in winter in North Florida.

Now for the bad, ugly-behaving Clerodendrums: the fragrant, pink flowers of Cashmere Bouquet (*C. bungei*) belie its extremely aggressive nature. Don't plant it unless you can contain it. Likewise for Tree Clerodendrum (*C. trichotomum*), which produces suckers that will spread 30–50 feet, and *C. quadriloculare*, Starburst Clerodendrum, which grows 12–15 feet tall and suckers far from the original plant. This plant's showy purple leaves and large beautiful flowers are enticing . . . but beware. The dwarf cultivar 'Morningstar' is purportedly less aggressive. A variegated form of *C. quadriloculare* also exists. Another species to avoid in tropical areas is Chinese Glory Bower (*C. chinensis, C. fragrans, C. philippinum*).

Java Glory Bower

Pride of Burma Clerodendrum

Starburst Clerodendrum

Latin name: *Cuphea ignea*

Common name: Cigar Flower

Hardiness zones: 9a–11

Plant form/height: upright, spreading/2–3 feet

Florida native: no (Mexico, West Indies)

Cold tolerance: tender

Flower color/season: pink to purple; yellow-orange to scarlet/spring, summer, fall

Leaf color/texture: dark green/fine to medium

Light: sun

Soil: well drained, organic, acid, somewhat drought tolerant

Salt tolerance: low

Pest problems: metallic beetles; otherwise pest free

Uses: mid-border; attracts butterflies/hummingbirds

Method of propagation: seed and cuttings

Narrative: The lance-shaped leaves and small tubular flowers of Cigar Flower provide textural interest. Pinch or prune during the warm months to maintain a dense shape; otherwise it becomes leggy. Attracts hummingbirds and butterflies. Giant Cigar Flower (*C. micropetala*) grows to 6 feet and produces multicolored orange to yellow flowers in fall and spring.

Latin name: *Dianthus caryophyllus*

Common name: Perennial Dianthus

Hardiness zones: 8a–9a

Plant form/height: rounded/6–10 inches; flowers to 24 inches

Florida native: no (Mediterranean)

Cold tolerance: hardy

Flower color/season: pinks, purples, reds, white/fall, winter, spring

Leaf color/texture: dark green/medium

Light: sun to part shade

Soil: very well drained, organic, acid, somewhat drought tolerant

Salt tolerance: medium

Pest problems: generally pest free

Uses: massing, cut flower

Method of propagation: seed, cuttings

Narrative: Requires frequent deadheading in spring; may look unsightly in hot/humid weather. *D. chinensis*, sold as a cool season annual, will often live through the summer if provided a little shade.

Latin name: *Dietes iridioides* (syn. *D. vegeta*)

Common name: African Iris

Hardiness zones: 8b–11

Plant form/height: upright, clumping/24 inches; flowers to 36 inches

Florida native: no (South Africa)

Cold tolerance: hardy

Flower color/season: white/fall, winter, spring

Leaf color/texture: light green/coarse

Light: sun to part shade

Soil: well drained, acid or alkaline pH, very drought tolerant

Salt tolerance: low

Pest problems: generally pest free

Uses: massing, accent plant, mid-border

Method of propagation: division, seedlings

Narrative: Low maintenance plant. Iris-like foliage adds interest to garden.

Latin name: *Duranta erecta*

Common name: Golden Dewdrop

Hardiness zones: 9a–11

Plant form/height: upright/4–6 feet

Florida native: yes

Cold tolerance: tender

Flower color/season: blue, white, purple/summer, fall

Leaf color/texture: medium green/medium

Light: sun to part shade

Soil: well drained, drought tolerant

Salt tolerance: medium

Pest problems: generally pest free

Uses: accent plant; attracts butterflies/hummingbirds

Method of propagation: cuttings, seed

Narrative: Golden yellow berries are toxic to humans but eaten by birds. Cultivars include *D. erecta* 'Dwarf'; white flowering 'Alba'; purple flowered 'Sapphire Showers'; dwarf, lime green 'Compacta Aurea' and variegated forms

Latin name: *Echinacea purpurea*

Common name: Coneflower

Hardiness zones: 8a–9a

Plant form/height: rounded/6–12 inches; flowers to 12–18 inches

Florida native: yes

Cold tolerance: hardy

Flower color/season: purple/summer, fall

Leaf color/texture: dark green/coarse

Light: sun to part shade

Soil: rich, well drained, acid, somewhat drought tolerant

Salt tolerance: medium

Pest problems: fungal leaf spots, powdery mildew

Uses: massing, cut flowers; attracts butterflies

Method of propagation: seed

Narrative: Remove blooms as they fade to encourage more flowers. Excellent fresh cut or dried flowers. Short lived in Central Florida. May reseed. Orange, white, and yellow cultivars are available.

Latin name: *Eranthemum pulchellum*

Common name: Blue Sage

Hardiness zones: 9a–11

Plant form/height: rounded/4–6 feet

Florida native: no (India)

Cold tolerance: tender

Flower color/season: rich blue/winter

Leaf color/texture: dark green/coarse

Light: part shade to shade

Soil: fertile, moist, but well drained

Salt tolerance: medium

Pest problems: generally pest free

Uses: massing, back of border, accent plant

Method of propagation: cuttings

Narrative: Because of its short flowering period, Blue Sage should be used as a foil against more colorful, longer-blooming plants. However, its intense blue flowers are a welcome site in winter. Prune during the spring and summer to develop a short, dense plant.

Painted Elephant Ear

Elephant Ears Are Tropical, Easy, and Rewarding!

Elephant Ear is the common name for a group of plants that provide tropical texture and are generally hardy throughout the state. Care should be taken in selecting both the location for your plantings and the type of Elephant Ear you choose; a few members of this group have rampantly spread into natural areas. *As a general rule, these plants should not be planted in or near natural waterways.* However, don't be afraid to try them elsewhere; the right Elephant Ear in the right place will be one of the most striking perennials in your garden.

Plants in the genus *Colocasia* reproduce in wet areas by suckering vigorously and colonizing shoreline and boggy areas. *Colocasia esculenta* is very invasive in many regions of Florida. As a general rule, keep *Colocasia* in containers and do not plant them in wet areas. Some beautiful *Colocasia* that make wonderful

'Lime Zinger' Xanthosoma

'Lime Zinger' Xanthosoma, 'Portodora' Alocasia, 'Nancy's Revenge' Colocasia

Ruffled Elephant Ear, Wendt's Alocasia

Alocasia species

container specimens include 'Black Magic,' with its matte black foliage, and 'Cranberry' or 'Rhubarb,' which has gray leaves and reddish stalks.

Alocasia is generally not as cold hardy as *Colocasia*; hardiness varies with species. The good news is that *Alocasia* plants do not sucker, they clump, so they do not pose the invasive problems of *Colocasia*. The leaves of *Alocasia* are usually glossy and many are brightly colored and veined. For tough, cold-tolerant tropical color try *Alocasia plumbea* 'Rubra' with its 3–4-foot, glossy, plum violet leaves and stems. Looking for really giant leaves? Try *A.* x *portora*

'Portodora' (upright leaves to five feet or more), and *A. calodora* (upright leaves to six feet). For South Florida try *A.* x *amazonica* (glossy green black leaves with silver veins), *A.* 'Corozon' (glossy silver leaves to three feet in length), *A.* 'Hilo Beauty,' with spotted leaves in black brown and green, which grows to four feet in height, *A. sinuata* (leaves to five feet with wavy margins), and *A.* 'Frydek' (velvety green-black leaves with white veins).

Xanthosoma is a lesser known group of Elephant Ears that have a clumping growth habit and matte-colored leaves. Some outstanding forms have bright lime green leaves, such as 'Golden Delicious' and 'Lime Zinger.' Also look for *X. jeoquinii lineatum*, which has crested leaves with white striations and an upright habit. For containers and indoor use try *X. lindenii* 'Magnificum' (silvery and green leaves and a very aristocratic look).

Last but not least, don't forget Caladiums. Though they are a different group of plants they provide vibrant, long lasting color for shady or sunny Florida landscapes. There are hundreds of cultivars—big-leaved, small-leaved, lance-leaved—and new colors are emerging all the time.

Latin name: *Erigeron karvinskianus* 'Profusion'

Common names: Fleabane, Mexican Daisy
Hardiness zones: 8a–10
Plant form/height: ground cover, spreading/6–12 inches
Florida native: no (Mexico to Panama)
Cold tolerance: hardy
Flower color/season: white to pink/year-round
Leaf color/texture: gray-green/fine
Light: sun to part shade
Soil: very well drained, drought tolerant
Salt tolerance: medium
Pest problems: generally pest free
Uses: massing, front of border, wall or paving crevices
Method of propagation: cuttings, division
Narrative: This underused perennial blooms sporadically year-round, offering many small (3/4 inch) white daisylike flowers with yellow centers. Its fine-textured foliage contrasts nicely with other perennials. Reseeds.

Latin name: *Euryops pectinatus*

Common names: Bush Daisy, African Daisy Bush
Hardiness zones: 9a–10a
Plant form/height: rounded/12–24 inches
Florida native: no (South Africa)
Cold tolerance: semi-hardy
Flower color/season: yellow/spring, summer, fall
Leaf color/texture: green and gray-green/fine
Light: sun to part shade
Soil: well drained, acid or alkaline, somewhat drought tolerant
Salt tolerance: high
Pest problems: generally pest free
Uses: massing, mid-border; attracts butterflies
Method of propagation: cuttings
Narrative: Can be used in difficult situations. This plant is often confused with *Gamolepis chrysanthemoides.*

Latin name: *Evolvulus glomeratus*

Common name: Blue Daze
Hardiness zones: 9–11
Plant form/height: ground cover/6–10 inches
Florida native: no (western U.S.)
Cold tolerance: tender
Flower color/season: blue/year-round
Leaf color/texture: silver-green/fine
Light: sun to part shade
Soil: well drained, acid or alkaline, somewhat drought tolerant
Salt tolerance: medium to high
Pest problems: fungal leaf spots
Uses: massing, front of border
Method of propagation: cuttings
Narrative: A fungal blight sometimes causes Blue Daze to die back during warm, wet summer months. Fortunately, the plant grows fast and usually recovers from the problem.

Latin name: *Gaillardia pulchella*

Common name: Blanket Flower
Hardiness zones: 8a–11
Plant form/height: rounded, ground cover/6 inches; flowers to 24 inches
Florida native: yes (or possibly naturalized)
Cold tolerance: hardy
Flower color/season: yellow and reds/year-round
Leaf color/texture: light green/coarse
Light: sun
Soil: very well drained, very drought tolerant, tolerates poor and highly alkaline soils
Salt tolerance: high
Pest problems: generally pest free
Uses: massing, cut flowers, wildflower garden; attracts butterflies
Method of propagation: division, seed
Narrative: *Gaillardia* is perfectly suited to coastal gardens. Many cultivars exist. Shade or overly moist soils will cause *Gaillardia* to rot. This plant is usually short lived, but readily reseeds.

Tropical and Fragrant: Don't Forget the Gingers

'Elisabeth' Hedychium

One of the joys of gardening in the South is finding plants with a tropical look and, if possible, a tropical fragrance. While not all of the gingers are fragrant, their diversity, durability, and beauty are exceeded only by their ease of growing. No matter where you live in the state of Florida there are gingers that will provide a unique aspect to your landscape.

Hedychium—the fragrant Butterfly Gingers are the only gingers with a strong fragrance. The beautiful waxy blooms come in white, pink, orange, and red tones. In North Florida they die back to the ground each year, but in South Florida they provide a permanent green foliage mass. Peak flowering is in the late spring and summer.

Zingiber—The Pine Cone Gingers have a unique short flower stalk that emerges from the ground green and reddens as the season progresses. The rich liquid found in the blossoms is credited with being a burn lotion, insect repellent, and shampoo. The tropical green foliage is striking and the plant is extremely hardy throughout the state.

'Pink V' Hedychium

Curcuma—The Hidden Gingers have bold bananalike foliage; some have colorful markings or tones. The flowers of curcuma are brilliantly colored conelike structures in jewel tones of orange, purple, cerise, and white to shades of green. Some species flower before the leaves emerge from the soil in spring (hence hidden gingers) and others like *C. roscoeana* bear their flowers at the top of the plant later in the season. Either way, these are striking plants and fully hardy across the state.

Peacock Ginger

Globba—The Dancing Ladies Gingers are usually less than three feet in height. The flowers are borne in graceful arcs from the tips of the stems. Beautifully colored bracts twirl around the stalks like small dancing ladies in shades of burgundy, yellow, lavender, and white. Small rhizomes form on the stems of some species and make wonderful pass-along plants for friends to grow.

Costus—The Spiral Gingers are a tropical group of ginger relatives with beautiful flowers and stems that often have a spiral twist, hence the common name. Flower color ranges from orange to yellow and into deep reds. Leaves are green, purple, or variegated. Central and South Floridians really need to try this rewarding group of plants.

Kaempferia—Peacock Gingers are a shade-loving group of plants with leaves beautifully marked in purples and greens overlaid with reflective silver patterns. The leaves disappear in winter and reappear in spring. In Florida, the Peacock Gingers provide a substitute for *Hosta*, which does not perform well in the state. Flowering characteristics vary by species but the smaller forms (*K. pulchra*) bloom throughout the summer with star-shaped two-inch blooms in pink, lavender, or white tones. Larger species like *K. grande* and *K. rotunda* bloom before foliage emerges and small clusters of pink flowers look like fallen boutonnieres. The genus *Cornukaempferia* resembles the Peacock Gingers but has a larger leaf and bright orange flowers.

Variegated Shell Ginger

Alpinia—The Torch and Shell Gingers have perhaps the most strikingly tropical flowers but are best suited to the southern half of the state. Alpinia are evergreen forms of the ginger family and, while they may live in the northern part of the state, require a frostfree winter to bloom. Bold foliage textures and large bloom spikes make them a South Florida favorite. *A. purpurata* is a true tropical torch ginger and dies to the ground at around 50°F. *A. zerumbet*, Shell Ginger, is somewhat more cold tolerant but *A. zerumbet* 'Variegata,' with bright yellow stripes over green leaves, is grown extensively for its strong tropical effect in the landscape.

Blue Ginger (*Dichorisandra thyrsiflora*) is not a true ginger; it is actually a relative of the common houseplant called Wandering Jew. Its flowers provide a wonderful late summer splash of deep royal blue color. For South Floridians this plant is almost a woody shrub. In North Florida it dies to the ground each winter, but is easily rooted from stem cuttings. Try Blue Ginger in part shade and enjoy the blooms from August through fall in frostfree regions of the state.

Other ginger relatives include *Heliconia* (see the Perennial Selection Guide) and banana.

Blue Ginger

Latin name: *Gaura lindheimeri*

Common name: Whirling Butterflies

Hardiness zones: 8a–9a

Plant form/height: rounded/12 inches; flowers to 24–30 inches

Florida native: no (Texas, Louisiana)

Cold tolerance: tender

Flower color/season: white or pink/spring, summer, fall

Leaf color/texture: gray-green/medium

Light: sun

Soil: acid or alkaline, drought tolerant

Salt tolerance: low

Pest problems: leaf-spot fungi, powdery mildew

Uses: mid border, massing

Method of propagation: seed

Narrative: The delicate pinkish white flowers on long stems add a light and airy look to the perennial garden. Do not move once planted; *Gaura* has a deep carrotlike root that does not transplant well. Forms include pink flowers and variegated leaves.

Latin name: *Gerbera jamesonii*

Common name: Gerbera Daisy

Hardiness zones: 8b–11

Plant form/height: rounded/6 inches; flowers to 10–12 inches

Florida native: no (Africa)

Cold tolerance: tender

Flower color/season: pink, yellow, white, orange, red, rose/year-round

Leaf color/texture: dark green/coarse

Light: sun to part shade

Soil: well drained, organic, acid, somewhat drought tolerant

Salt tolerance: high

Pest problems: powdery mildew fungus, slugs and snails

Uses: massing, cut flowers; attracts butterflies

Method of propagation: division, seed

Narrative: Keep the crown of the plant slightly above ground level to prevent fungal rot. Dig and divide Gerbera Daisies when plants become crowded or when the crown of the plant sinks into the soil. Plants should be protected from frost, which will damage foliage.

Latin name: *Glandularia tampensis*
(Verbena tampensis)

Common names: Tampa Verbain, Tampa Mock Vervain
Hardiness zones: 9a–11
Plant form/height: rounded/2–3 feet
Florida native: yes
Cold tolerance: hardy
Flower color/season: lavender/winter, spring
Leaf color/texture: medium green/medium
Light: sun to part shade
Soil: moist
Salt tolerance: medium to high
Pest problems: generally pest free
Uses: massing, wildflower garden; attracts butterflies
Method of propagation: cuttings
Narrative: May reseed.

Latin name: *Hamelia patens*

Common name: Firebush
Hardiness zones: 8a–11
Plant form/height: rounded/4–6 feet
Florida native: yes
Cold tolerance: tender
Flower color/season: red-orange/warm months
Leaf color/texture: light green/medium
Light: sun to part shade
Soil: wide range, acid or alkaline, very drought tolerant
Salt tolerance: medium
Pest problems: generally pest free
Uses: back of border, accent plant; attracts butterflies/
hummingbirds
Method of propagation: seed, cuttings, air layer
Narrative: Flowers are followed by 1/4 inch, purple-
black berries that are eaten by a number of birds.
Where no winter damage occurs, Firebush will require
pruning to keep it bushy and in scale. Fertilize
sparingly.

Latin name: *Helianthus angustifolius*

Common names: Swamp Sunflower/Narrow-leaf Sunflower

Hardiness zones: 8a–9a

Plant form/height: upright/4–6 feet

Florida native: yes

Cold tolerance: hardy (dormant in winter)

Flower color/season: yellow/fall

Leaf color: dark green/coarse

Light: sun to part shade

Soil: well drained, acid or alkaline, tolerates wet and dry

Salt tolerance: unknown

Pest problems: powdery mildew, rust, spittlebugs

Uses: back of border, massing, wildflower garden; attracts butterflies

Method of propagation: division, seed

Narrative: If grown in part shade, pinch plants twice in early summer to encourage branching. Heavy feeders. Many plantlets develop around base; divide yearly. Often reseeds.

Latin name: *Helianthus debilis*

Common name: Beach Sunflower

Hardiness zones: 8a–11

Plant form/height: ground cover/6–10 inches

Florida native: yes

Cold tolerance: tender

Flower color/season: yellow/year-round

Leaf color/texture: bright green/medium

Light: sun

Soil: well drained, acid or alkaline, very drought tolerant

Salt tolerance: high

Pest problems: generally pest free

Uses: ground cover, wildflower garden; attracts butterflies

Method of propagation: cuttings

Narrative: Reseeds from year to year. This plant can be aggressive in the garden.

Latin name: *Heliconia* species

Common name: Lobster Claw

Hardiness zones: 9a–11

Plant form/height: upright, spreading/1–15 feet depending on type

Florida native: no (Central and South America, southwestern Pacific)

Cold tolerance: semi-hardy

Flower color/season: orange, red, pink, or yellow/ warm months

Leaf color/texture: variable by type/coarse

Light: sun to part shade

Soil: tolerant of wet and well-drained soils, acid or alkaline, somewhat drought tolerant

Salt tolerance: medium

Pest problems: generally pest free

Uses: mid- or back of border (depending on type), massing, cut flowers, accent plant

Method of propagation: division, seed

Narrative: Protect from wind. Can spread several feet. *Heliconia* imparts an unmistakable tropical look to the garden, but should not be considered a low mainte-nance plant.

Latin name: *Heliotropium angiospermum*

Common names: Scorpion-tail Heliotrope, Butterfly Heliotrope

Hardiness zones: 9a–11

Plant form/height: rounded/3 feet

Florida native: yes

Cold tolerance: tender

Flower color/season: white/year-round

Leaf color/texture: dark green/coarse

Light: sun to part shade

Soil: tolerates drought and flooding

Salt tolerance: low to medium

Pest problems: generally pest free

Uses: mid-border, transition plant, wildflower garden; attracts butterflies

Method of propagation: cuttings, seed

Narrative: The small flowers of Scorpion-tail are not particularly showy, but its durable nature and crinkled, dark green foliage make it an interesting addition to the perennial garden. Readily reseeds. *H. amplexi-caule*, the non-native Spreading Heliotrope, has purple flowers; ground cover form; dies back in winter.

Latin name: *Hemerocallis* hybrids

Common name: Daylily

Hardiness zones: 8a–10

Plant form/height: rounded, clumping, ground cover/
6–12 inches, flowers up to 36 inches

Florida native: no (China, Korea, Japan)

Cold tolerance: semi-hardy

Flower color/season: yellows, reds, pinks, or purples/
late spring

Leaf color/texture: light to medium green/medium

Light: sun to part shade

Soil: well drained, fertile, organic, acid, somewhat
drought tolerant, but prefers moisture

Salt tolerance: medium to high

Pest problems: nematodes, Daylily Rust disease

Uses: front- or mid-border, massing, ground cover

Method of propagation: division, seed

Narrative: Some varieties are evergreen, while others
are deciduous. Each flower lasts only one day. A wide
range of flower colors, petal shapes, and plant heights
exist. The American Hemerocallis Society can provide
detailed information on this diverse plant.

Latin name: *Hemigraphis* species

Common names: Dragon's Breath, Waffle Plant, Red
Flame Ivy

Hardiness zones: 9b–11

Plant form/height: ground cover/6–12 inches

Florida native: no (Malaysia)

Cold tolerance: tender

Flower color/season: flowers are not showy

Leaf color/texture: purple and red/fine to medium

Light: sun to part shade

Soil: organic, moist

Salt tolerance: none to low

Pest problems: mealybug

Uses: front of border, massing

Method of propagation: seed and cuttings

Narrative: Many forms with beautiful foliage. *H.
coloratus* has purple leaves overlaid with silver.

Latin name: *Hibiscus* species

Common names: Hibiscus, Mallow, Turk's Cap
Hardiness zones: 8–11
Plant form/height: upright, rounded/4–10 feet depending on type
Florida native: some species
Cold tolerance: variable by species; see Narrative
Flower color/season: variable/variable
Leaf color/texture: medium green/fine to coarse
Light: sun
Soil: variable by type
Salt tolerance: high
Pest problems: caterpillars, grasshoppers
Uses: back of border, accent plant, wildflower garden, water garden; attracts butterflies/hummingbirds
Method of propagation: cuttings, seed
Narrative: See Hibiscus: Bold and Colorful (pages 57–59) for more information.

Latin name: *Hosta* species

Common name: Hosta
Hardiness zones: 8a–8b
Plant form/height: rounded, ground cover/1–2 feet; flowers up to 18 inches
Florida native: no (Japan, China, hybrid origin)
Cold tolerance: hardy (dormant in winter)
Flower color/season: white, lavender/summer
Leaf color/texture: variable by type/coarse
Light: part shade to shade
Soil: moist, rich, organic
Salt tolerance: unknown
Pest problems: slugs
Uses: massing, accent plant, ground cover
Method of propagation: division
Narrative: Hostas are best suited only to the most northern areas of Florida. Good Hosta substitutes for Florida are the Peacock Gingers (see *Kaempferia* for more information). See also Very Shade Tolerant Perennials under Plants for Special Uses and Conditions at the end of this chapter.

Hibiscus: Bold and Colorful

The signature of tropical landscapes from Hawaii to Florida is the hibiscus. Different types of hibiscus are available to satisfy gardeners across the state:

Tropical Hibiscus—Almost everyone is familiar with the tropical hibiscus (*H. rosa-sinensis*) and the rainbow of colorful flowers that are available. New colors continue to emerge from the Hibiscus Society's avid breeders. Also look for *H.* 'Snow Queen,' with beautifully variegated foliage that looks best in full hot sun. This plant is a reliable Central Florida perennial and a woody tree in South Florida but is usually damaged by North Florida's cold winters.

Hardy Hibiscus—In North and Central Florida, look to the hardy hibiscus group (*Hibiscus mosheutos* and its hybrids). These cold tolerant forms have a winter dormancy requirement and may not perform well in South Florida. Huge flowers up to 12 inches across and a long flowering season make hybrids such as 'Disco Belle,' 'Lava,' 'Old Yella,' and 'Lord Baltimore'

Unnamed Hibiscus Hybrid

very rewarding to grow. New hybrids are emerging constantly with flower colors ranging from deep purple through red, pink, white, and muted yellows. Hardy hibiscus types die to the ground each year, sprout back up in late spring, and flower in summer.

Unnamed Hibiscus Hybrid

'Disco Belle Pink' Hibiscus

Hibiscus: Bold and Colorful
continued

Confederate Rose Hibiscus

Hibiscus mutabilis

'Lady Baltimore' Hibiscus

Also try these hibiscus relatives:

H. mutabilis—the Confederate Rose, a small treelike form with double flowers that open white and fade to pink.

Turk's Cap (*Malvaviscus drummondii*)—a hardy species with small red flowers held upright. A larger, common form (*Malvaviscus arboreus*) has 2–3-inch flowers in red, pink, or white. The bell-shaped flowers are strong hummingbird attractors. This plant is woody in Central and South Florida but occasionally freezes back in North Florida.

'Gator Pride' Hibiscus

Scarlet Hibiscus

Abutilon—Flowering Maple (*Abutilon hybridum*), with foliage resembling maple leaves, is not a maple at all but a strong, low-growing shrub of the hibiscus family best for Central Florida and southward, where they provide cool season color. Wonderful bell-like flowers in shades of red, yellow, orange, pink, white, and bi-colors hang from the stems. Peak bloom is in spring and fall. *A. pictum* 'Thompsonii' has attractive yellow-green mottled foliage and *A.* 'Souvenir de Bonn' has beautifully variegated white and green foliage (see *Abutilon* in the Perennial Selection Guide).

The Rosemallows—These tough native plants grow throughout Florida, usually in marshy areas. *H. coccineus*, Scarlet Hibiscus, produces beautiful red flowers in summer. The Saltmarsh Mallow (*Kosteletzkya virginica*) has pink flowers and will tolerate salty conditions. Swamp Rosemallow (*H. grandiflorus*) can be seen along Florida's coast and inland areas as well. The Rosemallows die to the ground in winter but return in spring for early summer flowering.

Flowering Maple

Flowering Maple

'Bella' Flowering Maple

Latin name: *Hypoestes phyllostachya*

Common name: Polka Dot Plant
Hardiness zones: 8b–11, annual in 8a
Plant form/height: ground cover/6–12 inches
Florida native: no (Madagascar)
Cold tolerance: tender
Flower color/season: flowers not showy
Leaf color/texture: pink, red, or white, depending on type/medium
Light: part shade to shade
Soil: well drained, organic, acid, somewhat drought tolerant
Salt tolerance: none
Pest problems: generally pest free
Uses: front of border, massing, container
Method of propagation: seed, cuttings
Narrative: Bright light intensifies the foliage color and speckling, but full sun is too harsh. Plants often reseed, but seedlings often have inferior foliage.

Latin name: *Ipomoea batatas*

Common name: Ornamental Sweet Potato
Hardiness zones: 8a–11
Plant form/height: ground cover/6–12 inches
Florida native: no (Central America, Pacific Islands)
Cold tolerance: tender
Flower color/season: flowers not showy
Leaf color/texture: variable by type/coarse
Light: sun
Soil: well drained, organic, acid, somewhat drought tolerant
Salt tolerance: unknown
Pest problems: whitefly
Uses: ground cover (seasonal), container
Method of propagation: cuttings
Narrative: These plants are fast growers and demand a lot of room. Many cultivars exist with purple-black, chartreuse, bronze, and variegated leaves

Latin name: *Iris* species and hybrids

Common names: Louisiana Iris (hybrids), Blue Flag, and others

Hardiness zones: 8a–10b

Plant form/height: upright, spreading/18–24 inches; flowers up to 36 inches

Florida native: some species

Cold tolerance: semi-hardy

Flower color/season: blue, red, white, yellow, pink, bronze, or purple/spring

Leaf color/texture: dark green/medium

Light: sun to part shade

Soil: moist, organic, acid

Salt tolerance: unknown

Pest problems: generally pest free

Uses: mid-border, massing, cut flowers, accent plant, water gardens

Method of propagation: division, seed

Narrative: Swordlike leaves and rhizomatous roots. May perform better as bog or water garden plants in southern regions. Heirloom varieties may prove to be the hardiest. Bearded Iris and Japanese Iris do not perform well in Florida.

Latin name: *Justicia brandegeana*

Common name: Shrimp Plant

Hardiness zones: 8b–11

Plant form/height: rounded/4 feet

Florida native: no (Mexico)

Cold tolerance: tender

Flower color/season: reddish brown bracts with white flowers/warm months

Leaf color/texture: medium green/medium

Light: sun to part shade

Soil: rich, organic, moist

Salt tolerance: none

Pest problems: generally pest free

Uses: accent plant, massing; attracts butterflies/ hummingbirds

Method of propagation: cuttings, division

Narrative: Also known as *Beloperone guttata*. Rapid grower. The flower bracts of the cultivar 'Jambalaya' are a warm red; 'Chartreuse'—bracts are lime green; 'Yellow Queen'—bracts are glowing yellow; 'Fruit Cocktail' is a pink, green, and yellow-bracted cultivar.

Latin name: *Justicia carnea*

Common names: Jacobinia, Flamingo Flower, Brazilian Plume

Hardiness zones: 8b–11

Plant form/height: upright/3–4 feet

Florida native: no (South America)

Cold tolerance: tender

Flower color/season: rose or white/spring, summer, fall

Leaf color: medium green/coarse

Light: part shade to shade

Soil: well drained, acid, somewhat drought tolerant

Salt tolerance: none

Pest problems: generally pest free

Uses: mid- or back of border, massing

Method of propagation: cuttings

Narrative: Weak plant in North Florida. Drops its leaves when temperatures get near freezing. Prune heavily each year to keep bushy. Requires frequent deadheading. Other *Justicia* worth trying are *J. betonica* (White Shrimp Plant), *J. pectoralis* (Tilo), *J. spicigera* (Orange Plume), *J. aurea*, *J. fulvicoma*, and *J. coccinea*. Closely related genera are *Pachystachys* and *Dicliptera*.

Latin name: *Kaempferia* species

Common name: Peacock Ginger

Hardiness zones: 8a–11

Plant form/height: ground cover, spreading/6–36 inches depending on type

Florida native: no (Asia)

Cold tolerance: hardy (dormant in winter)

Flower color/season: lavender and white/spring, summer

Leaf color/texture: patterned or variegated/medium to coarse

Light: part shade to shade

Soil: wide range

Salt tolerance: none to low

Pest problems: generally pest free

Uses: ground cover (seasonal), Hosta replacement

Method of propagation: seed and division

Narrative: Deciduous in winter. *K. pulchra*—large succulent leaves, many colors and hybrids, pink to lavender flowers all summer; *K. masoniana*—smaller leaved, but similar to *K. pulchra*; *K. robusta*—18–24 inches, deep burgundy and silver leaves, flowers in spring before leaves emerge; *K. grande*—also spring flowering, leaves to 36 inches, green, purple, and silver patterned, very striking and hardy across the state. For additional information on Gingers see Tropical and Fragrant: Don't Forget the Gingers (pages 56–59).

Latin name: *Lantana* species

Common name: Lantana

Hardiness zones: 8a–11

Plant form/height: ground cover, rounded, upright depending on type/variable

Florida native: yes (some species; others native to tropical America, Australia, South Africa)

Cold tolerance: tender

Flower color/season: red, pink, orange, yellow, white/warm season

Leaf color: medium green/coarse

Light: sun

Soil: well drained, acid or alkaline, very drought tolerant

Salt tolerance: medium to high

Pest problems: whitefly, leaf spot fungus disease

Uses: massing, ground cover (depending on type); attracts butterflies/hummingbirds

Method of propagation: cuttings

Narrative: Butterflies adore the flowers and birds are attracted to the berries (which are poisonous to humans and livestock). One species, *L. camara*, has naturalized throughout Florida and is considered invasive. Improved cultivars are exceptional garden plants, but heavily fruiting cultivars should be avoided because of their invasive potential. For additional information, see Lantana: Marvel or Menace? (pages 64–65).

'Samantha' Lantana

Lantana: Marvel or Menace?

Lantana has sparked great debate in the plant world. On one hand, it is prized for its bold colors, herbal properties, drought and salt tolerance, and attraction to butterflies, song birds, and hummingbirds. On the other, it is scorned for its weedy nature and its potential disruption of habitat and wildlife ecology. Considered a pioneer species, the non-native *L. camara* has become naturalized throughout the state and is considered invasive. This plant is from tropical America, Australia, and/or South Africa, but because it reseeds easily and is a food source for birds, it is difficult to determine whether man or nature brought it to Florida's shores. "Old" forms of *L. camara* were bushy, upright, and very weedy. The flowers of *Lantana camara* may be multi-hued or solid colored; pollinated flowers change color to a darker hue. Most of

Purple Trailing Lantana

'Morning Glow' Lantana

'Miss Huff' Lantana

the commercial hybrids currently sold in nurseries are derived from breeding programs that use *L. camara* as a parent. Improved new cultivars are more mounding in habit and less prone to set seed. *L.* 'Gold Mound,' also called 'New Gold,' produces the least seed. The leaves and green immature fruits of *L. camara* are reported to be poisonous to livestock and humans.

Several species of lantana are native to Florida. *L. depressa* has bright yellow flowers and *L. involucrata* has small whitish flowers and an upright branching form. These natives make attractive landscape plants but can be difficult to find.

Non-native forms include *L. montevidensis*, commonly called Weeping Lantana, with a prostrate form and lavender flowers. There is also a white form, 'Alba.' *L. triloba* has lavender flowers on an upright plant and is a heavy seed producer. This species tends to be found more in North Florida.

'Gold Mound' Lantana

Latin name: *Leonotis leonurus*

Common name: Lion's Ear
Hardiness zones: 8a–11
Plant form/height: upright/4–5 feet
Florida native: no (South Africa)
Cold tolerance: tender
Flower color/season: orange/fall, winter, spring
Leaf color/texture: medium green/coarse
Light: sun
Soil: well drained
Salt tolerance: none to low
Pest problems: generally pest free
Uses: back of border, accent plant; attracts butterflies
Method of propagation: cuttings
Narrative: The large height and width of Lion's Ear demands room in the garden, but the unusual whorls of orange flowers are worth the space.

Latin name: *Leucanthemum superbum*

Common name: Shasta Daisy
Hardiness zones: 8a–9b
Plant form/height: rounded, clumping/6–8 inches; flowers to 2–3 feet
Florida native: no (Spain, France)
Cold tolerance: hardy
Flower color/season: white/spring
Leaf color/texture: dark green/coarse
Light: sun
Soil: well drained, acid, organic, not drought tolerant
Salt tolerance: none
Pest problems: generally pest free
Uses: mid-border, massing, cut flower
Method of propagation: division
Narrative: Look for local varieties that perform well in your area.
{Photo 3.2.52}

Latin name: *Lysimachia* species

Common name: Creeping Jenny

Hardiness zones: 8a–9a

Plant form/height: ground cover/2–6 inches

Florida native: no (eastern North America)

Cold tolerance: hardy

Flower color/season: yellow/year-round

Leaf color/texture: green or yellow green/medium

Light: sun to part shade

Soil: fertile, well drained

Salt tolerance: unknown

Pest problems: generally pest free

Uses: front of border, ground cover, water gardens

Method of propagation: cuttings

Narrative: *L. nummularia* 'Aurea' (Golden Creeping Jenny) is a variegated form. Hybrids of *L. congestiflora* produce bright yellow flowers on burgundy to green foliage. Cultivar 'Outback Sunset' is variegated white, red and yellow; cultivar 'Golden Harvest' has chartreuse and white variegation.

Latin name: *Monarda punctata*

Common names: Horsemint, Spotted Bee Balm

Hardiness zones: 8a–10b

Plant form/height: rounded/2–3 feet

Florida native: yes

Cold tolerance: tender

Flower color/season: pale lavender/summer, fall

Leaf color: light green/medium

Light: sun

Soil: sandy, well drained, acid or alkaline, very drought tolerant

Salt tolerance: medium to high

Pest problems: generally pest free

Uses: mid-border, massing, wildflower garden; attracts butterflies/hummingbirds

Method of propagation: division, cuttings, seed

Narrative: Found from Long Island south to Florida. *Monarda didyma* or Bee Balm is sometimes grown as a short-lived perennial in Florida; it does not usually tolerate hot/humid conditions. Look for heirloom varieties. May reseed.

Latin name: *Neomarica* species

Common name: Walking Iris
Hardiness zones: 9b–11
Plant form/height: rounded, clumping, ground cover/ 2–3 feet
Florida native: no (Brazil)
Cold tolerance: tender
Flower color/season: white and blue or yellow/spring, summer, fall
Leaf color/texture: light green/medium
Light: part shade to shade
Soil: wide range, acid, organic, somewhat drought tolerant
Salt tolerance: low
Pest problems: generally pest free
Uses: massing, container
Method of propagation: plantlets, division, seed
Narrative: *Neomarica caerulea* has white or very light blue petals with darker blue inner segments. *N. longifolia* has yellow flowers with brown/mahogany markings on the petals. Walking Iris propagate themselves through plantlets that form at the tips of the flower stalks, bend to the ground, and then take root.

Latin name: *Nierembergia caerulea*

Common name: Cup Flower
Hardiness zones: 8a–10
Plant form/height: ground cover/8 inches
Florida native: no (Argentina)
Cold tolerance: hardy
Flower color/season: white or blue/spring, summer, fall
Leaf color/texture: medium green/fine
Light: sun to part shade
Soil: well drained, organic
Salt tolerance: medium
Pest problems: generally pest free
Uses: front of border, massing, container
Method of propagation: cuttings
Narrative: The white cultivar 'Mont Blanc' and the rich, violet blue 'Purple Robe' perform well in Florida. Does best in containers.

Latin name: *Odontonema cuspidate*
(syn. *O. strictum*)

Common name: Firespike
Hardiness zones: 9a–11
Plant form/height: upright/4–6 feet
Florida native: no (Central America)
Cold tolerance: tender
Flower color/season: red/fall, winter in Central Florida; year-round in South Florida
Leaf color/texture: dark green/coarse
Light: sun to part shade
Soil: wide range, acid or alkaline, somewhat drought tolerant
Salt tolerance: low
Pest problems: generally pest free
Uses: back of border, massing, accent plant, cut flowers; attracts butterflies/hummingbirds
Method of propagation: cuttings
Narrative: Prune several times during the growing season to reduce height. *O. callistachyum* resembles Firespike except that the blooms are purple and produced January–February.

Latin name: *Orthosiphon stamineus*

Common name: Cat's Whiskers
Hardiness zones: 9b–11
Plant form/height: upright/2–3 feet
Florida native: no (eastern Asia)
Cold tolerance: tender
Flower color/season: white or pale lavender/year-round
Leaf color/texture: dark green/medium
Light: sun to part shade
Soil: moist, fertile, organic
Salt tolerance: none to low
Pest problems: generally pest free
Uses: mid-border, accent plant; attracts butterflies/hummingbirds
Method of propagation: cuttings
Narrative: The spikes of flowers with their elongated stamens are lovely and interesting. Prone to iron deficiency.

Latin name: *Otacanthus azureus*

Common name: Brazilian Snapdragon
Hardiness zones: 10–11
Plant form/height: upright/2–3 feet
Florida native: no (Brazil)
Cold tolerance: hardy
Flower color/season: blue/spring, fall
Leaf color/texture: medium green/medium
Light: sun to part shade
Soil: organic, rich, moist
Salt tolerance: unknown
Pest problems: generally pest free
Uses: mid-border, cut flowers
Method of propagation: cuttings
Narrative: May not survive periods of intense cold. 'Caribbean Blue' is an improved cultivar.

Latin name: *Pachystachys lutea*

Common names: Yellow Shrimp Plant, Lollipop Plant
Hardiness zones: 9a–11
Plant form/height: upright/3–5 feet
Florida native: no (Peru)
Cold tolerance: tender
Flower color/season: white with golden yellow bracts/ spring, summer, fall
Leaf color/texture: dark green/coarse
Light: part shade to shade
Soil: well drained, acid, somewhat drought tolerant
Salt tolerance: none
Pest problems: generally pest free
Uses: back of border, massing, accent plant; attracts butterflies
Method of propagation: cuttings
Narrative: Even where it remains unscathed by winter frosts, it should be pruned back hard in early spring. Cardinal's Guard (*P. coccinea*) is also quite shade tolerant, produces red blooms year-round in South Florida, and is cultivated similarly to Yellow Shrimp Plant.

Latin name: *Pedilanthus tithymaloides*

Common name: Devil's Backbone

Hardiness zones: 9b–11

Plant form/height: upright/2–3 feet

Florida native: no (tropical Americas)

Cold tolerance: tender

Flower color/season: small, red/winter

Leaf color/texture: green or variegated/coarse

Light: sun to shade

Soil: well drained, very drought tolerant

Salt tolerance: medium

Pest problems: generally pest free

Uses: massing, accent plant, container

Method of propagation: cuttings

Narrative: The upright, zigzag stems of *Pedilanthus* provide an interesting focal point in the perennial garden. Variegated forms are particularly distinctive. The milky sap of *Pedilanthus* is mildly poisonous if ingested and very irritating to the skin and eyes.

Latin name: *Pentas lanceolata*

Common name: Pentas

Hardiness zones: 8a–10a

Plant form/height: rounded/12–36 inches depending on type

Florida native: no (Arabian Peninsula, tropical Africa, Madagascar)

Cold tolerance: tender

Flower color/season: red, rose, pink, lilac, white, blue/year-round

Leaf color/texture: medium green/medium

Light: sun to part shade

Soil: well drained, acid, somewhat drought tolerant

Salt tolerance: low

Pest problems: generally pest free; nematodes

Uses: mid- to back of border, massing, cut flowers; attracts butterflies/hummingbirds

Method of propagation: cuttings

Narrative: Many new Pentas cultivars exist. Old-fashioned, unnamed varieties are often hardier perennials, are more attractive to butterflies, and do not require deadheading like some new types.

Latin name: *Peristrophe hyssopifolia*
'Aureo-variegata'

Common name: Marble Leaf
Hardiness zones: 9a–10b
Plant form/height: ground cover/1 foot
Florida native: no (Java)
Cold tolerance: tender
Flower color/season: lavender/winter
Leaf color/texture: yellow and green/medium
Light: sun to part shade
Soil: well drained
Salt tolerance: unknown
Pest problems: generally pest free
Uses: ground cover
Method of propagation: cuttings
Narrative: Yellow variegation increases in full sun, fades in shade. Tiny purple flowers are a bonus.

Latin name: *Phlox* species

Common name: Phlox
Hardiness zones: 8a–9a
Plant form/height: species dependent; see Narrative
Florida native: yes (*P. divaricata*); Texas, eastern United States, Canada
Cold tolerance: hardy
Flower color/season: species dependent (see below)
Leaf color/texture: light green/fine
Light: sun to part shade
Soil: well drained, acid, somewhat drought tolerant
Salt tolerance: unknown
Pest problems: generally pest free
Uses: front- or mid-border, massing, butterfly attractor
Method of propagation: division, cuttings
Narrative: *P. divaricata* (Woodland Phlox) is a native, low-growing species with blue flowers in early spring; plant in a sunny location. *P. paniculata* (Garden Phlox) is upright (2–3 feet) and its magenta flowers appear in summer and fall; *P. subulata* (Creeping Phlox) is very dwarf (3–4 inches) and spreading; pink, blue, and lavender forms exist; blooms in April and May.

Latin name: *Physostegia virginiana*

Common names: False Dragon Head, Obedient Plant
Hardiness zones: 8a–9b
Plant form/height: spreading; upright when in flower/ 8 inches; flowers to 36 inches
Florida native: no (North America); native species exist
Cold tolerance: semi-hardy
Flower color/season: lavender, white or pink/fall
Leaf color/texture: light green/medium
Light: sun to part shade
Soil: tolerates wet or dry, acid or alkaline
Salt tolerance: unknown
Pest problems: generally pest free
Uses: mid-border, massing, cut flowers; attracts hummingbirds
Method of propagation: division, seed
Narrative: Stake or support weak flower stems. Spreads by seed and underground runners and can become a nuisance. 'Summer Snow' and 'Miss Manners' are less aggressive. The name "Obedient Plant" is derived from the fact that the flowers remain in place when turned on the stem.

Latin name: *Plectranthus* species

Common name: Plectranthus
Hardiness zones: 9b–11, annual in zones 8a–9a
Plant form/height: rounded, upright or ground cover depending on type/variable
Florida native: no (South Africa)
Cold tolerance: semi-hardy
Flower color/season: white, purple, or pink/summer, fall, or intermittent
Leaf color/texture: green, gray, or variegated/medium
Light: sun to part shade
Soil: rich, organic, moist
Salt tolerance: low to moderate
Pest problems: mealybug, spider mites
Uses: front or mid-border color; ground cover, container
Method of propagation: cuttings
Narrative: Many different forms. See Plectranthus: Old and New Favorites (pages 74–75).

Creeping Variegated Plectranthus

Plectranthus: Old and New Favorites

Swedish Ivy (*Plectranthus australis*), with its sturdy green foliage and vining stems, has graced homes and patios as a durable house-plant or hanging basket plant for many years. Now, however, new and improved cultivars of plectranthus have emerged as ground covers, outstanding container plants, and/or flowering perennials for the garden.

Foliage types offer an array of leaf colors and variegations. Gray Plectranthus (*P. argentatus*) has fuzzy silver stems and an upright growth habit to 36 inches. Creeping Coleus (*P. madagascariensis*) forms a trailing ground cover with green leaves edged in cream to white. Cuban Oregano, also known as 'Athens Gem' (*P. amboinicus*), produces a 14-inch mound of thick, fuzzy leaves with a variety of leaf colors. The foliage is fragrantly spicy. Forster's Plectranthus (*P. forsteri*) grows upright to 36 inches and has green leaves with big cream

Cuban Oregano

Mixed Plectranthus at the University of Florida's trial gardens in Gainesville

'Cape Angels' and 'Sky Symphony' Plectranthus

colored edges. The striking golden-yellow leaves of 'Gold Coin' (*P. ciliatus*) have green centers. The plant grows to 24 inches. Plectranthus 'Nicoletta' (*P. tomentosus*) has attractive spreading silver-gray foliage and spikes of royal blue flowers.

Flowering types produce numerous sprays of white, pink, blue, or lavender blooms in late summer and fall. Some, like Mona Lavender (*P.* hybrid) with its profuse and elegant lavender flowers, bloom intermittently. Mona Lavender has a compact, upright growth habit and dark green leaves tinged with purple undersides that are typical of many plectranthus species. The foliage of Purple Smelly Dog Plant (*P. ecklonii*) has somewhat offensive-smelling foliage when bruised, but its 5-foot, shrublike habit and fall flowers make up for it. Blue, pink, and white cultivars are available. The ground cover form of Zulu Wonder (*P. zuluensis*) grows quickly to 18 inches tall and 3 feet across. Beautiful purple flowers are held on 5-inch spikes above the quilted, rich green leaves.

Forster's Variegated Plectranthus

'Silver Shield' and "Smelly Dog" Plectranthus

'Silver Shield' and 'Mona Lavender' Plectranthus

'Irma' Plectranthus

Latin name: *Plumbago auriculata*

Common name: Plumbago
Hardiness zones: 8a–11
Plant form/height: rounded/3–6 feet
Florida native: no (South Africa)
Cold tolerance: tender
Flower color/season: light blue, sky blue, white/year-round
Leaf color/texture: medium green/medium
Light: sun to part shade
Soil: wide range, somewhat drought tolerant
Salt tolerance: low
Pest problems: generally pest free
Uses: back of border, massing; attracts butterflies/hummingbirds
Method of propagation: cuttings, division
Narrative: *Plumbago* is at its best when allowed to be a loose, unclipped shrub. However, a hard prune may occasionally be necessary to increase its bushiness and flowering. *Plumbago scandens* (Florida Leadwort) is a low growing, spreading Florida native that produces small white flowers in fall.

Latin name: *Pseuderanthemum laxifolia*

Common names: Amethyst Star, Shooting Star
Hardiness zones: 9b–11
Plant form/height: upright/2–3 feet
Florida native: no (tropics)
Cold tolerance: tender
Flower color/season: lavender/fall
Leaf color/texture: medium green/medium
Light: sun to part shade
Soil: well drained, organic
Salt tolerance: unknown
Pest problems: generally pest free
Uses: back of border, accent plant
Method of propagation: cuttings
Narrative: A variegated form, *Pseuderanthemum variegata* (Key West Snow Bush), has attractive cream and green foliage and fewer flowers and is also more shade tolerant. It is easily injured by frost and best suited to South Florida.

Latin name: *Rondeletia leucophylla*

Common name: Rondeletia
Hardiness zones: 9b–11
Plant form/height: rounded/3 feet
Florida native: no (tropical America)
Cold tolerance: semi-hardy
Flower color/season: rose/winter, spring
Leaf color/texture: green-gray/fine to medium
Light: sun to part shade
Soil: tolerant of poor soils
Salt tolerance: low
Pest problems: generally pest free
Uses: massing, accent plant; attracts butterflies
Method of propagation: cuttings
Narrative: Prone to iron deficiency. *R. splendens* is called the Panama Rose. Its large, scarlet clusters of flowers look nothing like roses, although the plant's graceful arching habit resembles old-fashioned rose varieties. *R. splendens* is not hardy in North Florida.

Latin name: *Rudbeckia* species

Common names: Black-eyed Susan, Brown-eyed Susan, Gloriosa Daisy
Hardiness zones: 8a–9b
Plant form/height: rounded, clumping/6–12 inches; flowers up to 3 feet
Florida native: yes, eight species
Cold tolerance: tender
Flower color/season: yellow/summer, fall
Leaf color/texture: medium to dark green/coarse
Light: sun
Soil: well drained, very drought tolerant
Salt tolerance: low
Pest problems: fungal foliage diseases
Uses: mid-border, massing, cut flowers; attracts butterflies
Method of propagation: seed, division, cuttings
Narrative: Heat tolerant; 'Goldsturm' is a good cultivar for North Florida. *R. triloba* is a good performer, but short lived in Central Florida. Fuzzy-leafed types are more susceptible to fungus diseases. Some species reseed.

Latin name: *Ruellia* species

Common names: Ruellia, Mexican Petunia, Florida Petunia, more

Hardiness zones: 8b–10b

Plant form/height: upright or rounded/1–3 feet depending on type

Florida native: five species (tropical America, warm parts of North America, Africa, Asia)

Cold tolerance: semi-hardy

Flower color/season: blue, red, pink, white, or violet/ many species bloom year-round

Leaf color/texture: variable by type

Light: sun to part shade

Soil: well drained, acid or alkaline, very drought tolerant

Salt tolerance: low to moderate

Pest problems: generally pest free

Uses: front or back of border, massing, ground cover (depending on type), wildflower garden; attracts butterflies

Method of propagation: division, cuttings, seed

Narrative: Ruellia are survivors under adverse growing conditions. Many species readily reseed. *R. brittoniana* (syn. *R. tweediana*) spreads aggressively by underground runners and seed and is considered very invasive. 'Purple Showers' is a sterile, preferred cultivar. The Dwarf Mexican Petunia, *R. brittoniana* 'Katie,' is less aggressive and makes a nice ground cover. Flower colors include white, pink, and blue. *R. caroliniensis* (Florida Petunia) is a blue-flowered Florida native. *R. elegans* (Brazilian Ruellia) is a spreading ground cover with deep red flowers in warm months.

Latin name: *Russelia equisetiformis*

Common names: Firecracker Plant, Coral Plant
Hardiness zones: 9–12
Plant form/height: rounded/3 feet
Florida native: no (Mexico)
Cold tolerance: tender
Flower color/season: red or pale yellow/year-round
Leaf color/texture: bright green/fine
Light: sun to part shade
Soil: well drained, somewhat drought tolerant
Salt tolerance: medium
Pest problems: generally pest free
Uses: massing, accent plant, container; attracts butterflies/hummingbirds
Method of propagation: division, tip cuttings
Narrative: Give this plant plenty of room to sprawl and spread. *R. sarmentosa* is more upright and the red flowers more substantial.

Latin name: *Salvia* species

Common names: Salvia, Sage
Hardiness zones: 8–10
Plant form/height: rounded or upright/2–6 feet depending on type
Florida native: yes, some species
Cold tolerance: variable by species
Flower color/season: red, blue, white, lavender, coral, burgundy, pink, or yellow/variable by type
Leaf color/texture: variable by type
Light: sun to part shade
Soil: wide range, somewhat drought tolerant
Salt tolerance: poor to low
Pest problems: generally pest free
Uses: mid- to back of border, massing, accent plant, some culinary uses; attracts butterflies/hummingbirds
Method of propagation: seed, cuttings, division
Narrative: A large and diverse group of plants. No perennial garden should be without some. See Those Splendid Salvias (pages 80–82) for more information.

Those Splendid Salvias

Few perennials offer the diversity of salvias and no Florida flower garden should be without some. Flower colors range from the deepest blue to lavender, red, yellow, and white. Salvias also vary widely in size and leaf shape and texture.

As a group, the perennial salvias that perform best in Florida require full sun to light shade. They are normally tolerant of Florida soil and drought conditions. However, occasional watering during dry times will increase flowering and vigor. Many grow tall and are best used in the back of the perennial bed or as specimen plants. Some, like *Salvia coccinea*, bloom almost year-round. Others flower in fall and/or spring when night temperatures are cooler. Salvias should be pruned after flowering or as needed to maintain their shape and size. With time, the stems of *Salvia* can become woody; do not prune into this woody growth.

Several culinary salvias grow in Florida: Sage (*Salvia officinalis*), Greek Sage (*S. fruticosa*) and Pineapple Sage (*S. elegans*). The dried leaves of *S. greggii* can be used as seasoning and the flowers are great for salads and garnishes. All make nice additions to the Florida herb or perennial garden. Many salvias are also attractive to hummingbirds and butterflies, but not all salvias thrive in Florida. For best results, start with the ones listed here and then experiment.

Forsythia Sage (close up)

Salvia mexicana

Scarlet Sage

Mexican Sage (*Salvia leucantha*) is adapted to sunny, dry areas. It is also quite salt tolerant. This tall-growing plant can easily become 4 feet tall and wide. The lavender and white flower parts are furry and soft and held on 6-inch stems above the silver gray foliage. Although they bloom best in the sun, they also blossom in light shade. Several varieties are available in different shades of purple. Prune this salvia to the ground in winter, then lightly prune as it emerges and grows to produce a sturdy, branched plant.

Bog Sage (*Salvia uliginosa*) hails from South Africa and can spread aggressively from underground runners. The flowers produced in summer on this 3–4-foot plant are the purest sky blue. Bog Sage responds well to a hard prune in late spring.

Majestic Sage (*Salvia guaranitica*) is a slow-growing, beautiful salvia from South America. 'Black and Blue' has large, deep blue flowers enhanced by black calyxes. 'Argentine Skies' offers pale blue flowers. Both bloom off and on throughout the late spring and summer, tolerate light shade, and require moderate moisture.

Mexican Sage

Indigo Spires (*Salvia farinacea* x *longispicata*) is cold hardy and grows to 3–4 feet tall and wide. Its sprawling habit requires staking or some sort of support (tomato cages work great!). The beautiful, indigo blue flowers are striking, long lasting, and attractive to pollinating insects. Indigo Spires is quite cold tolerant and flowers year-round.

Bog Sage

Indigo Spires

Those Splendid Salvias *continued*

Tropical Sage (*Salvia coccinea*) is native to Florida, but improved cultivars like 'Lady in Red,' 'Snow Nymph,' and 'Coral Nymph' are showier. It can be killed back in North and Central Florida, but will reseed or resprout from the roots. Several color varieties can be found—from the well-known brilliant red to white, peach, and pink. Occasional irrigation increases its performance.

Van Hout's Sage

Also try Van Hout's Sage (*Salvia splendens Van Houttii*) with cranberry colored blooms, or one of its many hybrids: 'Paul'—purple flowers; 'Caribbean Coral'—coral blooms; 'Louis's Delight'—red; Forsythia Sage (*Salvia madrensis*)—large yellow flowers; Belize Sage (*Salvia miniata*)—bright red flowers and glossy foliage; and Autumn Sage (*Salvia greggii*)—a drought-tolerant species flowering in shades of red, pink, coral, and white.

Louis' Delight Sage

Autumn Sage

Latin name: *Sanchezia nobilis*

Common name: Sanchezia
Hardiness zones: 9b–11
Plant form/height: upright/up to 8 feet in South Florida
Florida native: no (tropical rainforests in Central and South America)
Cold tolerance: tender
Flower color/season: yellow/summer
Leaf color/texture: green with yellow and red striping/coarse
Light: sun to shade
Soil: rich, well drained
Salt tolerance: medium
Pest problems: spider mites occasionally
Uses: back of border, massing, accent plant, container
Method of propagation: cuttings
Narrative: Very tropical in appearance.

Latin name: *Schaueria flavicoma*

Common name: Golden Plume
Hardiness zones: 8b–11
Plant form/height: upright/24 inches
Florida native: no
Cold tolerance: semi-hardy
Flower color/season: yellow and white/spring, summer
Leaf color/texture: medium green/coarse
Light: part shade to shade
Soil: organic, rich, moist
Salt tolerance: unknown
Pest problems: spider mites, mealybug
Uses: massing, container; attracts butterflies
Method of propagation: cuttings, seed
Narrative: Nice medium-sized flowering plant, tolerant of heat and humidity. Yellowing leaves indicate an iron deficiency.

Latin name: *Scutellaria* species
Common name: Skull Cap
Hardiness zones: 8b–11
Plant form/height: upright or ground cover/12–18 inches depending on type
Florida native: yes, and also commercial hybrids.
Cold tolerance: semi-hardy
Flower color/season: blue, purple to red orange/year-round
Leaf color/texture: dark to gray green/fine to medium
Light: part shade
Soil: organic, rich
Salt tolerance: unknown
Pest problems: spider mites, mealybug
Uses: front of border, massing, wildflower garden; attracts butterflies
Method of propagation: seed, cuttings
Narrative: *Scutellaria costa-ricana*—upright to 24 inches, orange flowers with yellow tips; *S. formosana*—deep blue flowers on grayish foliage, very hardy; cultivars 'Pink Fountain' and 'Purple Fountain' are popular as hanging basket plants and low growing border plants.

Latin name: *Sedum* species
Common names: Sedum, Stonecrop
Hardiness zones: 8a–9a
Plant form/height: rounded, upright or ground cover/ variable with type
Florida native: no (Europe, Asia)
Cold tolerance: hardy
Flower color/season: yellow, also purple and red tones /spring
Leaf color/texture: variable by type
Light: sun to part shade in South Florida
Soil: sandy, infertile, very well drained, drought tolerant
Salt tolerance: medium
Pest problems: diseases associated with too much rain or irrigation
Uses: front of border, massing, container; attracts butterflies
Method of propagation: cuttings
Narrative: All succulents need dry conditions, good air circulation, and well-drained soil. They struggle in Florida's hot, wet summers. Use only gravel as mulch. Once established, they require low water and low fertilization. Try Stonecrop (*S. acre*); Autumn Joy Sedum (*S. spectabile* 'Autumn Joy'); *S.* 'Frosty Morn'; Dragon's Blood Sedum (*S. spurium*) and *S. mexicanum*.

Latin name: *Solidago* species

Common name: Goldenrod

Hardiness zones: 8a–11

Plant form/height: upright, spreading/1–4 feet depending on type

Florida native: yes (some species)

Cold tolerance: hardy (dormant in winter)

Flower color/season: yellow/fall

Leaf color/texture: dark green/medium

Light: sun to part shade

Soil: wide range, acid or alkaline, very drought tolerant

Salt tolerance: high

Pest problems: generally pest free

Uses: back of border, cut flower, wildflower garden; attracts butterflies

Method of propagation: division, seed

Narrative: Goldenrod is often blamed for allergies when in fact it is nonallergenic (i.e., ragweed is usually the culprit). Many native species exist and dwarf cultivars are commercially available. May reseed.

Latin name: *Stachytarpheta* species

Common name: Porterweed

Hardiness zones: 9a–11

Plant form/height: upright/6 inches to 6 feet depending on type

Florida native: one species (*S. jamaicensis*)

Cold tolerance: tender

Flower color/season: dark and light blues, coral, red, purple/warm months

Leaf color/texture: dark green/coarse

Light: sun to part shade

Soil: well drained, drought tolerant

Salt tolerance: medium to high

Pest problems: generally pest free

Uses: massing or accent plant (depending on type); attracts butterflies/hummingbirds

Method of propagation: cuttings

Narrative: Prune to keep plant in proportion to its setting. Reblooms quickly after pruning. Reseeds readily.

Latin name: *Stokesia laevis*

Common name: Stokes Aster

Hardiness zones: 8a–11

Plant form/height: rounded, clumping/6 inches; flowers to 1 foot

Florida native: yes

Cold tolerance: semi-hardy

Flower color/season: blue, white, purple, pink, yellow/ spring, fall

Leaf color/texture: dark green/medium

Light: sun to part shade

Soil: wide range, acid, somewhat drought tolerant

Salt tolerance: low to moderate

Pest problems: generally pest free

Uses: front of border, massing, cut flowers, wildflower garden; attracts butterflies

Method of propagation: division

Narrative: Water and fertilize frequently when growing Stokes Aster in full sun; purple/blue forms are best known; cultivars offer other colors.

Latin name: *Strelitzia reginae*

Common name: Bird of Paradise

Hardiness zones: 9b–11

Plant form/height: upright, clumping/3–4 feet

Florida native: no (South Africa)

Cold tolerance: semi-hardy

Flower color/season: orange and blue/summer, fall

Leaf color/texture: gray-green/coarse

Light: sun to part shade

Soil: well drained, acid or alkaline, somewhat drought tolerant

Salt tolerance: none

Pest problems: generally pest free

Uses: mid-border, massing, accent plant, cut flowers

Method of propagation: division, seed

Narrative: Slow growing; prefers low, steady levels of nitrogen.

Latin name: *Strobilanthes dyerianus*

Common name: Persian Shield

Hardiness zones: 9–11

Plant form/height: rounded/4 feet

Florida native: no (Myanmar)

Cold tolerance: tender

Flower color/season: pale blue/winter

Leaf color/texture: purple with silver/coarse

Light: part shade to shade

Soil: wide range

Salt tolerance: high

Pest problems: generally pest free

Uses: mid-border, massing, accent plant

Method of propagation: cuttings

Narrative: Foliage often becomes unattractive at flowering. Prune at this time and also lightly in summer to increase bushiness and sturdiness.

Latin name: *Talinum paniculatum* 'Variegata'

Common name: Jewels of Opar

Hardiness zones: 9a–11

Plant form/height: rounded to upright/3 feet

Florida native: no (southern U.S. to Central America)

Cold tolerance: tender

Flower color/season: pink/summer

Leaf color/texture: variegated/medium

Light: part shade to shade

Soil: rich, moist

Salt tolerance: unknown

Pest problems: generally pest free

Uses: mid-border, massing

Method of propagation: cuttings

Narrative: The variegated green and white foliage and delicate sprays of tiny pink flowers and yellow fruits make this plant a must for the shady perennial garden. *T. paniculatum* 'Aurea' has chartreuse foliage. The green form readily reseeds and is considered undesirable.

Latin name: *Tecoma stans*

Common names: Yellow Elder, Yellow Bells, Esperanza
Hardiness zones: 8b–11
Plant form/height: upright/variable by type and zone
Florida native: no (tropical America)
Cold tolerance: tender
Flower color/season: yellow/summer in North and Central Florida; year-round in South Florida
Leaf color/texture: medium green/coarse
Light: sun
Soil: well drained, drought tolerant
Salt tolerance: medium to high
Pest problems: generally pest free
Uses: back of border, accent plant; attracts hummingbirds
Method of propagation: cuttings, seed
Narrative: Very tolerant of heat and humidity.

Latin name: *Torenia* hybrids

Common name: Trailing Wishbone Flower
Hardiness zones: 10a–11
Plant form/height: ground cover/ 3–6 inches
Florida native: no (tropical Africa and Asia)
Cold tolerance: tender
Flower color/season: deep blue, purple, pink, white/ warm months
Leaf color/texture: medium green/medium
Light: part shade to shade
Soil: fertile, moist and well drained
Salt tolerance: poor
Pest problems: generally pest free
Uses: front of border, massing
Method of propagation: cuttings, seed
Narrative: Trailing Wishbone Flower is a perennial cultivar of *Torenia fournieri* (Wishbone Flower or Summer Pansy), a favorite annual for the summer garden.

Latin name: *Tulbaghia violacea*

Common name: Society Garlic

Hardiness zones: 8–10

Plant form/height: ground cover/12 inches

Florida native: no (South Africa)

Cold tolerance: semi-hardy

Flower color/season: lavender/spring, early summer

Leaf color/texture: gray-green/fine

Light: sun

Soil: well drained, drought tolerant

Salt tolerance: medium

Pest problems: generally pest free

Uses: front of border, massing, ground cover, cut flowers

Method of propagation: division (in winter)

Narrative: Society Garlic is a member of the onion family, The leaves emit a strong garlic smell when bruised, but some sources claim the flowers are fragrant at night. It will tolerate drought, but blooms best with moderate irrigation.

Latin name: *Turnera ulmifolia*

Common names: Cuban Buttercup, Yellow Alder

Hardiness zones: 9–11

Plant form/height: rounded/2 feet

Florida native: no (tropical America)

Cold tolerance: tender

Flower color/season: yellow or white/year-round

Leaf color/texture: bright green/coarse

Light: sun to part shade

Soil: well drained, drought tolerant

Salt tolerance: medium

Pest problems: generally pest free

Uses: front of border, massing

Method of propagation: cuttings

Narrative: Occasional light pruning is necessary to keep this plant neat and blooming. Often reseeds.

Upright Verbena

Variable Verbenas

Verbena species vary so much from one another that they warrant a little extra space in this book. For example, Upright Verbena grows to 4 feet, whereas trailing verbenas may reach only 4 inches and spread to 3-foot mats of foliage and flowers. Most verbenas tend to be quite drought tolerant and all are attractive to butterflies. They make wonderful additions of color to the garden—particularly in early spring.

Verbena x *hybrida* is a general group of verbena hybridized by cross-pollinating *Verbena canadensis* and many other species. This group makes a low-growing (5–8 inch) ground cover, but is a weak perennial in all but the northernmost parts of the state. Many new cultivars offer some disease resistance (powdery mildew is a major problem) and a wider palette of colors (red, white, salmon, lavender, purple, pink, and rose).

Verbena Hybrids

V. bonariensis (Upright Verbena), a native of South America that has naturalized across much of Florida, grows 4–5 feet tall. It makes a bold architectural statement in the perennial garden with its clusters of tiny, purple flowers borne on upright, square stems. *V. bonariensis* blooms throughout the summer and dies back in winter but normally resprouts or reseeds.

V. tenuisecta has more finely divided leaves and a very prostrate habit. Many of today's hybrids are crosses between *V. tenuisecta* and *V. canadensis*. Flower colors are lavenders and white.

Varieties of *V. rigida*, like 'Polaris' with its silver-lavender flowers, deserve a try. *Glandularia tampensis*, a first cousin of *Verbena*, is a Florida native plant that offers lavender flowers in winter. This plant and many other native *Glandularia* species are endangered, so please leave them where you find them in the wild. Tampa Verbain is available from plant nurseries.

Verbena bonariensis

Moss Verbena

Temari Purple Verbena

Latin name: *Verbena* species

Common name: Verbena
Hardiness zones: 8a–10b
Plant form/height: ground cover or upright/variable by type
Florida native: some species
Cold tolerance: semi-hardy
Flower color/season: lavender, red, pink, blue/spring, summer, fall
Leaf color/texture: light green/fine to coarse
Light: sun to part shade
Soil type: well drained, acid or alkaline, very drought tolerant
Salt tolerance: poor
Pest problems: generally pest free
Uses: massing, accent plant, cut flowers, ground cover (depending on species); attracts butterflies
Method of propagation: seed, cuttings
Narrative: A very diverse and tough group of plants. No butterfly garden should be without a verbena or two. See Variable Verbenas (pages 90–91).

Latin name: *Vernonia gigantea*

Common names: Ironweed, Giant Ironweed
Hardiness zones: 8a–9b
Plant form/height: upright/3–6 feet
Florida native: yes
Cold tolerance: hardy (dormant in winter)
Flower color/season: purple/summer, fall
Leaf color/texture: dark green/coarse
Light: sun to part shade
Soil: wide range, moist
Salt tolerance: unknown
Pest problems: generally pest free
Uses: back of border, accent plant, wildflower garden, water garden; attracts butterflies
Method of propagation: cuttings
Narrative: Prune several times in spring to produce a well-branched plant with more flowering stems. May need staking. Reseeds.

Latin name: *Vinca major*

Common names: Vinca, Periwinkle

Hardiness zones: 8a–8b

Plant form/height: ground cover/3–6 inches

Florida native: no (Europe)

Cold tolerance: hardy

Flower color/season: pale to intense sky blue/spring

Leaf color/texture: dark green or variegated/medium

Light: sun to part shade

Soil: organic, moist

Salt tolerance: poor

Pest problems: foliar fungal diseases

Uses: front of border, ground cover, hanging basket, container

Method of propagation: cuttings

Narrative: *V. major* 'Variegata'—gray-white leaves, grows rampantly; *V. major* 'Maculata'—green leaves marbled with yellow green, very strong, nice color; *V. major* 'Wojo's Gem'—striking white and green variegation, less vigorous than others. Most do not produce flowers in great numbers.

"Up and Comers"
for Florida Gardens

As this book goes to press, new perennials are emerging that hold great promise for Florida gardeners. Listed below are a few that have performed well in our yards and are easy to grow. Most are becoming available at retail garden centers. So here are a few newcomers to consider—no doubt other new, wonderful perennials will follow these!

St. Bernard's Lily

Cleome 'Linde Armstrong'

Bulbine

Anthericum sanderii: St. Bernard's Lily is a delightful little plant with great versatility for gardens in zones 8–10. The upright, grassy clumps of narrow leaves grow to about 2 feet tall and the delicate white flowers, which are produced nearly year-round, are held above the foliage. St. Bernard's Lily will grow in sun or shade. It performs best in moist but well-drained soils. Try it in mixed or mass plantings in the garden or grow it in a container as a combination plant or specimen.

Bulbine frutescens: The bright orange or yellow flowers of Bulbine make it a standout in the garden. It hails from the desert grasslands of South Africa, which makes it quite drought hardy but intolerant of wet conditions. It can be grown as a ground cover or container plant in full sun or light shade. Its succulent, grasslike leaves grow to 10–12 inches and form 2-foot clumps; flowers appear spring through summer and are held high above the foliage. It is hardy to heat and cold. 'Hallmark' is a sterile cultivar. Otherwise, Bulbine is propagated from seed and division.

Cleome 'Linde Armstrong': This compact (2-foot), thornless Cleome was selected and promoted as an outstanding annual, but it will persist as a perennial in Central and South Florida when winters are mild. Its short stature, delicate leaves, and lavender-pink flowers that appear nearly year-round make it a nice addition to any flower garden. It is extremely tolerant of heat and humidity. It will reseed, but not aggressively. Full sun or part shade is best. The blooms make nice cut flowers and are attractive to hummingbirds.

Dianella tasmanica: Flax Lily can be grown throughout the state in full sun or part shade and is quite durable. It forms 1–2-foot tall clumps of straplike leaves. Try 'Gold Stripe' for striking gold variegation and 'Variegata' for white-striped foliage. Small, delicate blue flowers are produced on wiry stems above the plant in winter and spring; these are followed by blueberrylike fruits. Dianella can be used as a ground cover, a specimen plant, or a handsome container plant. It divides easily.

Flax Lily

Farfugium japonicum: The common name, Leopard Plant, is derived from the fact that most cultivars of this plant have irregular cream or yellow markings. However, solid green leaf forms exist as well, and some have interesting ruffled or wavy margins. The large, leathery leaves are held on long stalks above the plant and can be 4–10 inches across. In fall or winter, the plant produces clusters of yellow daisylike flowers. Leopard Plant grows throughout Florida if provided a shady site and rich, moist soil whether in the ground or in a container.

Leopard Plant

Persicaria microcephala 'Red Dragon': Here's another undemanding plant that provides interesting foliage. 'Red Dragon' forms a 3-foot clump of upright, 2-foot red stems. The leaves are marked with burgundy and silver colors that vary with the season. Small white flowers are produced summer and fall. The foliage can be cut back at the end of winter to make way for the colorful new growth. It grows in zones 8 and 9 and perhaps farther south if provided shade. Unlike some invasive Persicaria species 'Red Dragon' is sterile and, although it is vigorous, it is not invasive.

'Red Dragon' Persicaria

3.3. Perennials for Special Uses and Conditions

A perennial exists for almost every landscape use and growing condition. The following lists will help you select the best plants for your purposes. Refer to the Perennial Selection Guide for additional information.

Perennials with Rounded Plant Form

Allamanda (*Allamanda cathartica* subspecies 'Schottii')

Aster (*Aster laevis*)

Begonia (*Begonia* species)

Black-eyed Susan (*Rudbeckia* species)

Blanket Flower (*Gaillardia pulchella*)

Blue Sage (*Eranthemum pulchellum*)

Brazilian Button Flower (*Centratherum punctatum*)

Bush Daisy (*Euryops pectinatus*)

Chrysanthemum (*Chrysanthemum grandiflora*)

Cleome 'Linde Armstrong' (*Cleome* 'Linde Armstrong')

Coneflower (*Echinacea purpurea*)

Crossandra (*Crossandra infundibuliformis*)

Cuban Buttercup (*Turnera ulmifolia*)

Daylily (*Hemerocallis* hybrids)

Dianthus (*Dianthus caryophyllus*)

Firebush (*Hamelia patens*)

Firecracker Plant (*Russelia equisetiformis*)

Gerbera Daisy (*Gerbera jamesonii*)

Golden Dewdrop (*Duranta repens* 'Dwarf' and 'Compacta Aurea')

Hibiscus (*Hibiscus* species)

Horsemint (*Monarda punctata*)

Jewels of Opar (*Talinum paniculatum* 'Variegata')

Joseph's Coat (*Alternanthera* species)

Lantana (*Lantana* species)

Leopard Plant (*Farfugium japonicum*)

Lily of the Nile (*Agapanthus* species)

Mexican Heather (*Cuphea hyssopifolia*)

Mistflower (*Conoclinium coelestinum*)

Pentas (*Pentas lanceolata*)

Persian Shield (*Strobilanthes dyerianus*)

Plectranthus (*Plectranthus* species)

Plumbago (*Plumbago auriculata*)

Red Dragon (*Persicaria microcephala* 'Red Dragon')

Rondeletia (*Rondeletia leucophylla*)

Ruellia (*Ruellia* species)

Salvia (*Salvia* species)

Scorpion-tail (*Heliotropium angiospermum*)

Sedum (*Sedum* species)

Shasta Daisy (*Leucanthemum superbum*)

Shrimp Plant (*Justicia brandegeana*)

Skull Cap (*Scutellaria* species)

Stokes Aster (*Stokesia laevis*)

Tampa Verbain (*Glandularia tampensis*)

Tropical Jasmines (*Cestrum* species)

Walking Iris (*Neomarica* species)

Whirling Butterflies (*Gaura lindheimeri*)

Wormwood (*Artemisia* species)

Yarrow (*Achillea* species)

Perennials with Upright Plant Form

African Iris (*Dietes iridioides*)

Alternanthera (*Alternanthera* 'Wave Hill')

Amethyst Star (*Pseuderanthemum laxifolia*)

Angelonia (*Angelonia angustifolia*)

Begonia (*Begonia* species)

Bird of Paradise (*Strelitzia reginae*)

Blackberry Lily (*Belamcanda chinensis*)

Brazilian Snapdragon (*Otacanthus azureus*)

Bulbine (*Bulbine frutescens*)

Cat's Whiskers (*Orthosiphon stamineus*)

Cigar Flower (*Cuphea ignea*)

Clerodendrum (*Clerodendrum species*)

Devil's Backbone (*Pedilanthus tithymaloides*)

Elephant Ear (*Alocasia, Colocasia, Xanthosoma* species)

False Dragon Head (*Physostegia virginiana*)

Firespike (*Odontonema cuspidata*)

Flax Lily (*Dianella tasmanica*)

Flowering Maple (*Abutilon hybridum*)

Gingers (*Hedychium* species)

Golden Dewdrop (*Duranta repens*)

Golden plume (*Schaueria flavicoma*)

Goldenrod (*Solidago* species)

Heliconia (*Heliconia* species)

Hibiscus (*Hibiscus* species)

Jewels of Opar (*Talinum paniculatum* 'Variegata')

Ironweed (*Vernonia gigantea*)

Jacobinia (*Justicia* carnea)

Lantana (*Lantana* species)

Lion's Ear (*Leonotis leonurus*)

Louisiana Iris (*Iris* species)

Milkweed (*Asclepias* species)

Philippine Violet (*Barleria cristata*)

Phlox (*Phlox* paniculata)

Plectranthus (*Plectranthus* species)

Porterweed (*Stachytarpheta* species)

Ruellia (*Ruellia brittoniana, R. sarmentosa*)

Salvia (*Salvia* species)

Sanchezia (*Sanchezia nobilis*)

Sedum (*Sedum* species)

Skullcap (*Scutellaria costa-ricana*)

St. Bernard's Lily (*Anthericum sanderii*)

Swamp Sunflower (*Helianthus angustifolius*)

Tropical Jasmines (*Cestrum* species)

Verbena (*Verbena bonariensis*)

Yellow Elder (*Tecoma stans*)

Yellow Shrimp Plant (*Pachystachys lutea*)

Perennials with Ground Cover Plant Form

Beach Sunflower (*Helianthus debilis*)

Begonia (*Begonia* species)

Blanket Flower (*Gaillardia pulchella*)

Blue Daze (*Evolvulus glomeratus*)

Bulbine (*Bulbine frutescens*)

Creeping Jenny (*Lysimachia nummularia*)

Cupflower (*Nierembergia caerulea*)

Daylily (*Hemerocallis* species)

Dragon's Breath (*Hemigraphis repanda*)

Flax Lily (*Dianella tasmanica*)

Fleabane (*Erigeron karvinskianus* 'Profusion')

Heliotrope (Spreading) (*Heliotropium amplexi-caule*)

Hosta (*Hosta* hybrids)

Joseph's Coat (*Alternanthera* species)

Lantana (*Lantana montevidensis*)

Marble Leaf (*Peristrophe hyssopifolia* 'Aureo-variegata')

Mexican Heather (*Cuphea hyssopifolia*)

Ornamental Sweet Potato (*Ipomoea batatas*)

Peacock Ginger (*Kaempferia* species)

Phlox (*P. divaricata, P. subulata*)

Plectranthus (*Plectranthus* species)

Polka Dot Plant (*Hypoestes phyllostachya*)

Red Dragon (*Persicaria* 'Red Dragon')

Ruellia (*R. elegans, R. brittoniana* 'Katie')

Sedum (*Sedum* species)

Skull Cap (*Scutellaria* species)

Society Garlic (*Tulbaghia violacea*)

Spreading Heliotrope (*H. amplexicaule*)

St. Bernard's Lily (*Anthericum sanderii*)

Torenia (*Torenia* hybrids)

Verbena (*Verbena* species)

Vinca major (*Vinca major*)

Walking Iris (*Neomarica* species)

Yarrow (*Achillea* species)

Perennials with Purple or Lavender Flowers

Allamanda (*Allamanda* species)

Amethyst Star (*Pseuderanthemum laxifolia*)

Angelonia (*Angelonia angustifolia*)

Aster (*Aster laevis*)

Brazilian Button Flower (*Centratherum punctatum*)

Cat's Whiskers (*Orthosiphon stamineus*)

Chrysanthemum (*Chrysanthemum grandiflora*)

Cigar Plant (*Cuphea ignea*)

Cleome 'Linde Armstrong' (*Cleome* 'Linde Armstrong')

Clerodendrum (*Clerodendrum* species)

Coneflower (*Echinacea purpurea*)

Cupflower (*Nierembergia caerulea*)

Daylily (*Hemerocallis* hybrids)

Dianthus (*Dianthus caryophyllus*)

False Dragon Head (*Physostegia virginiana*)

Firespike (*Odontonema callistachyum*)

Gingers (*Alpinia, Curcuma, Globba*)

Golden Dewdrop (*Duranta repens*)

Hibiscus (*Hibiscus* species)

Horsemint (*Monarda punctata*)

Hosta (*Hosta* species)

Ironweed (*Vernonia gigantea*)

Lantana (*Lantana montevidensis*)

Louisiana Iris (*Iris* species)

Marble Leaf (*Peristrophe hyssopifolia* 'Aureo-variegata')

Mexican Heather (*Cuphea hyssopifolia*)

Mistflower (*Conoclinium coelestinum*)

Peacock Ginger (*Kaempferia* species)

Pentas (*Pentas lanceolata*)

Philippine Violet (*Barleria cristata*)

Phlox (*Phlox subulata*)

Plectranthus (*Plectranthus* species)

Polka Dot Plant (*Hypoestes phyllostachya*)

Salvia (*Salvia* species)

Shrimp Plant (*Justicia brandegeana*)

Skullcap (*Scutellaria* species)

Society Garlic (*Tulbaghia violacea*)

Spreading Heliotrope (*Heliotropium amplexicaule*)

Stokes Aster (*Stokesia laevis*)

Tampa Verbain (*Glandularia tampensis*)

Torenia (*Torenia* hybrids)

Verbena (*Verbena* species)

Vinca major (*Vinca major*)

Perennials with Blue Flowers

African Iris (*Dietes iridioides*)

Angelonia (*Angelonia angustifolia*)

Aster (*Aster laevis*)

Bird of Paradise (*Strelitzia reginae*)

Blue Daze (*Evolvulus glomeratus*)

Blue Sage (*Eranthemum pulchellum*)

Brazilian Snapdragon (*Otacanthus azureus*)

Clerodendrum (*Clerodendrum ugandense*)

Cupflower (*Nierembergia caerulea*)

Flax Lily (*Dianella tasmanica*)

Golden Dewdrop (*Duranta repens*)

Gingers (*Kaempferia* species, *Dichorisandra thyrsiflora*)

Lily of the Nile (*Agapanthus* species)

Louisiana Iris (*Iris* species)

Mistflower (*Conoclinium coelestinum*)

Pentas (*Pentas lanceolata*)

Phlox (*Phlox divaricata*, *P. subulata*)

Plectranthus (*Plectranthus* species)

Plumbago (*Plumbago auriculata*)

Porterweed (*Stachytarpheta* species)

Ruellia (*Ruellia* species)

Salvia (*Salvia guaranitica*, *S. uliginosa*)

Skull Cap (*Scutellaria* species)

Stokes Aster (*Stokesia laevis*)

Torenia (*Torenia* hybrids)

Verbena (*Verbena* hybrids)

Walking Iris (*Neomarica* species)

Vinca major (*Vinca major*)

Perennials with Red Flowers

Begonia (*Begonia* species)

Blanket Flower (*Gaillardia pulchella*)

Cardinal's Guard (*Pachystachys coccinea*)

Chrysanthemum (*Chrysanthemum grandiflora*)

Cigar Flower (*Cuphea ignea*)

Clerodendrum (*Clerodendrum* species)

Crossandra (*Crossandra infundibuliformis*)

Daylily (*Hemerocallis* hybrids)

Devil's Backbone (*Pedilanthus tithymaloides*)

Dianthus (*Dianthus caryophyllus*)

Firebush (*Hamelia patens*)

Firecracker (*Russelia equisetiformis*, *R. sarmentosa*)

Firespike (*Odontonema cuspidata*)

Flowering Maple (*Abutilon hybridum*)

Gerbera Daisy (*Gerbera jamesonii*)

Gingers (*Hedychium*, *Zingiber*, *Costus*)

Heliconia (*Heliconia* species)

Hibiscus (*Hibiscus* species)

Lantana (*Lantana camara*)

Louisiana Iris (*Iris* species)

Milkweed (*Asclepias* species)

Panama Rose (*Rondeletia splendens*)

Pentas (*Pentas* lanceolata)

Porterweed (*Stachytarpheta coccinea*)

Red Cestrum (*Cestrum elegans*)

Ruellia (*Ruellia* species)

Salvia (*Salvia coccinea*, *S. splendens*, *S. miniata*)

Sedum (*Sedum* species)

Shrimp Plant (*Justicia brandegeana*)

Skullcap (*Scutellaria* species)

Verbena (*Verbena* hybrids)

Perennials with Orange or Coral Flowers

Barleria (*Barleria repens*)

Begonia (*Begonia* species)

Bird of Paradise (*Strelitzia reginae*)

Blackberry Lily (*Belamcanda chinensis*)

Blanket Flower (*Gaillardia pulchella*)

Bulbine (*Bulbine frutescens*)

Chrysanthemum (*Chrysanthemum grandiflora*)

Cigar Flower (*Cuphea ignea, C. micropetala*)

Clerodendrum (*Clerodendrum speciosissimum*)

Coneflower (*Echinacea purpurea*)

Crossandra (*Crossandra infundibuliformis*)

Daylily (*Hemerocallis* hybrids)

Firebush (*Hamelia patens*)

Flowering Maple (*Abutilon hybridum*)

Gerbera Daisy (*Gerbera jamesonii*)

Gingers (*Hedychium* species, *Curcuma* species, *Cornukaempferia*)

Heliconia (*Heliconia* species)

Hibiscus (*Hibiscus rosa-sinensis*)

Lantana (*Lantana camara*)

Lion's Ear (*Leonotis leonurus*)

Milkweed (*Asclepias* species)

Orange Plume (*Justicia spicigera*)

Porterweed (*Stachytarpheta mutabilis*)

Salvia (*Salvia splendens, S. coccinea, S. greggii*)

Shrimp Plant (*Justicia brandegeana*)

Skull Cap (*Scutellaria costa-ricana*)

Verbena (*Verbena* x *hybrida*)

Perennials with White Flowers

African Iris (*Dietes iridioides*)

Angelonia (*Angelonia angustifolia*)

Begonia (*Begonia* species)

Cat's Whiskers (*Orthosiphon stamineus*)

Clerodendrum (*Clerodendrum wallichii, C. thomsoniae*)

Coneflower (*Echinacea purpurea*)

Chrysanthemum (*Chrysanthemum grandiflora*)

Cuban Buttercup (*Turnera ulmifolia*)

Cupflower (*Nierembergia caerulea*)

Dianthus (*Dianthus caryophyllus*)

False Dragon Head (*Physostegia virginiana*)

Fleabane (*Erigeron karvinskianus* 'Profusion')

Flowering Maple (*Abutilon hybridum*)

Gerbera Daisy (*Gerbera jamesonii*)

Gingers (*Hedychium coronarium, Curcuma* species, *Globba* species)

Golden Dewdrop (*Duranta repens*)

Golden Plume (*Schaueria flavicoma*)

Hibiscus (*Hibiscus mosheutos, H. mutabilis*)

Hosta (*Hosta* species)

Jacobinia (*Justicia carnea, J. betonica*)

Lantana (*Lantana* species)

Lily of the Nile (*Agapanthus africanus* 'Alba')

Louisiana Iris (*Iris* species)

Mexican Heather (*Cuphea hyssopifolia*)

Milkweed (*Asclepias perennis*)

Mistflower (*Conoclinium coelestinum*)

Night Blooming Jasmine (*Cestrum nocturnum*)

Peacock Ginger (*Kaempferia* species)

Pentas (*Pentas lanceolata*)

Philippine Violet (*Barleria cristata*)

Plectranthus (*Plectranthus* species)

Plumbago (*Plumbago auriculata*)

Red Dragon (*Persicaria* 'Red Dragon')

Ruellia (*Ruellia* species)

Salvia (*Salvia leucantha, S. coccinea, S. greggii*)

Scorpion-tail (*Heliotropium angiospermum*)

Shasta Daisy (*Leucanthemum superbum*)

Shrimp Plant (*Justicia brandegeana*)

St. Bernard's Lily (*Anthericum sanderii*)

Stokes Aster (*Stokesia laevis*)

Verbena (*Verbena* hybrids)

Walking Iris (*Neomarica* species)

Whirling Butterflies (*Gaura lindheimeri*)

Yarrow (*Achillea* species)

Yellow Shrimp Plant (*Pachystachys lutea*)

Perennials with Yellow Flowers

Allamanda (*Allamanda cathartica*)

Beach Sunflower (*Helianthus debilis*)

Black-eyed Susan (*Rudbeckia* species)

Blanket Flower (*Gaillardia pulchella*)

Bulbine (*Bulbine frutescens*)

Bush Daisy (*Euryops pectinatus*)

Chrysanthemum (*Chrysanthemum grandiflora*)

Cigar Flower (*Cuphea* species)

Coneflower (*Echinacea purpurea*)

Creeping Jenny (*Lysimachia nummularia*)

Crossandra (*Crossandra infundibuliformis*)

Cuban Buttercup (*Turnera ulmifolia*)

Daylily (*Hemerocallis* hybrids)

Firebush (*Hamelia cuprea*)

Firecracker Plant (*Russelia equisetiformis*)

Flowering Maple (*Abutilon hybridum*)

Gerbera Daisy (*Gerbera jamesonii*)

Gingers (*Hedychium* hybrids, *Globba*, *Costus*)

Gold Cestrum (*Cestrum aurantiacum*)

Golden Plume (*Schaueria flavicoma*)

Goldenrod (*Solidago* species)

Heliconia (*Heliconia* species)

Hibiscus (*Hibiscus rosa-sinensis*)

Lantana (*Lantana* species)

Leopard plant (*Farfugium japonicum*)

Louisiana Iris (*Iris* species)

Milkweed (*Asclepias curassavica* 'Silky Gold')

Philippine Violet (*Barleria micans*)

Salvia (*Salvia madrensis*)

Stonecrop (*Sedum* species)

Shrimp Plant (*Justicia brandegeana* 'Aurea')

Stokes Aster (*Stokesia* hybrids)

Swamp Sunflower (*Helianthus angustifolius*)

Walking Iris (*Neomarica longifolia*)

Yarrow (*Achillea* species)

Yellow Elder (*Tecoma stans*)

Yellow Shrimp Plant (*Pachystachys lutea*)

Perennials with Pink or Rose Flowers

Angelonia (*Angelonia angustifolia*)

Begonia (*Begonia* species)

Chrysanthemum (*Chrysanthemum grandiflora*)

Clerodendrum (*Clerodendrum* species)

Daylily (*Hemerocallis* hybrids)

Dianthus (*Dianthus caryophyllus*)

False Dragon Head (*Physostegia virginiana*)

Fleabane (*Erigeron karvinskianus* 'Profusion')

Flowering Maple (*Abutilon hybridum*)

Gerbera Daisy (*Gerbera jamesonii*)

Gingers (*Hedychium* hybrids)

Heliconia (*Heliconia* species)

Hibiscus (*Hibiscus* species)

Jacobinia (*Justicia carnea*)

Jewels of Opar (*Talinum paniculatum* 'Variegata')

Lantana (*Lantana* species)

Louisiana Iris (*Iris* species)

Peacock Ginger (*Kaempferia* species)

Pentas (*Pentas lanceolata*)

Phlox (*Phlox subulata*)

Plectranthus (*Plectranthus* species)

Rondeletia (*Rondeletia leucophylla*)

Ruellia (*Ruellia* species)

Salvia (*Salvia* species)

Shrimp Plant (*Justicia brandegeana* 'Fruit Cocktail')

Skull Cap (*Scutellaria* species)

Stokes Aster (*Stokesia laevis*)

Torenia (*Torenia* hybrids)

Verbena (*Verbena* species)

Whirling Butterflies (*Gaura lindheimeri*)

Yarrow (*Achillea* species)

Perennials with Silver or Gray Foliage

Aster (*Aster laevis*)

Blue Daze (*Evolvulus glomeratus*)

Bush Daisy (*Euryops pectinatus*)

Chrysanthemum (*Ajania pacifica*)

Dianthus (*Dianthus caryophyllus*)

Elephant Ear (*Alocasia* and *Xanthosoma* species)

Heliotrope (*Heliotropium amplexicaule*)

Jewels of Opar (*Talinum paniculatum* 'Variegata')

Plectranthus (*Plectranthus* species)

Rondeletia (*Rondeletia leucophylla*)

Salvia (*Salvia leucantha*)

Skullcap (*Scutellaria* species)

Sedum (*Sedum* species)

Society Garlic (*Tulbaghia violacea*)

Vinca major (*Vinca major*)

Wormwood (*Artemisia* species)

Very Shade Tolerant Perennials

Begonia (*Begonia* species)

Blue Sage (*Eranthemum pulchellum*)

Crossandra (*Crossandra infundibuliformis*)

Devil's Backbone (*Pedilanthus tithymaloides*)

Elephant Ear (*Alocasia* species, *Xanthosoma* species)

Golden plume (*Schaueria flavicoma*)

Hosta (*Hosta* hybrids)

Jacobinia (*Justicia carnea*)

Jewels of Opar (*Talinum paniculatum* 'Variegata')

Leopard Plant (*Farfugium japonicum*)

Peacock Ginger (*Kaempferia* species)

Persian Shield (*Strobilanthes dyerianus*)

Polka Dot Plant (*Hypoestes phyllostachya*)

Red Dragon (*Persicaria* 'Red Dragon')

Sanchezia (*Sanchezia nobilis*)

Torenia (*Torenia* hybrids)

Walking Iris (*Neomarica* species)

Yellow Shrimp Plant (*Pachystachys lutea, P. coccinea*)

Perennials for Water Gardens or Wet Soil Conditions

Climbing Aster (*Aster carolinianus*)

Creeping Jenny (*Lysimachia nummularia*)

Elephant Ear (*Alocasia* species, *Colocasia* species)

Ginger (*Zingiber zerumbet*)

Heliconia (*Heliconia rostrata*)

Dragon's Breath (*Hemigraphis* species)

Hibiscus (*Hibiscus coccineus, H. grandiflorus*)

Ironweed (*Vernonia gigantea*)

Iris (*Iris* species)

Joseph's Coat (*Alternanthera* species)

Mexican Petunia (*Ruellia brittoniana*)

Milkweed (*Asclepias perennis*)

Mistflower (*Conoclinium coelestinum*)

Obedient Plant (*Physostegia virginiana*)

Salvia (*Salvia uliginosa*)

Swamp Sunflower (*Helianthus angustifolius*)

Walking Iris (*Neomarica* species)

Very Drought-Tolerant Perennials

African Iris (*Dietes iridioides*)

Beach Sunflower (*Helianthus debilis*)

Blackberry Lily (*Belamcanda chinensis*)

Black-eyed Susan (*Rudbeckia* species)

Blanket Flower (*Gaillardia pulchella*)

Brazilian Button Flower (*Centratherum punctatum*)

Bush Daisy (*Euryops pectinatus*)

Cigar Flower (*Cuphea ignea*)

Clerodendrum (*Clerodendrum* species)

Cuban Buttercup (*Turnera ulmifolia*)

Devil's Backbone (*Pedilanthus tithymaloides*)

Dianthus (*Dianthus caryophyllus*)

False Dragon Head (*Physostegia virginiana*)

Firebush (*Hamelia patens*)

Fleabane (*Erigeron karvinskianus* 'Profusion')

Golden Dewdrop (*Duranta repens*)

Goldenrod (*Solidago* species)

Heliotrope (*Heliotropium angiospermum*)

Horsemint (*Monarda punctata*)

Lantana (*Lantana* species)

Milkweed (*Asclepias curassavica*)

Porterweed (*Stachytarpheta* species)

Ruellia (*Ruellia* species)

Salvia (*Salvia leucantha, S. greggii*)

Sedum (*Sedum* species)

Society Garlic (*Tulbaghia violacea*)

Swamp Sunflower (*Helianthus angustifolius*)

Verbena (*Verbena* species, *Glandularia* species)

Whirling Butterflies (*Gaura lindheimeri*)

Wormwood (*Artemisia* species)

Yarrow (*Achillea* species)

Yellow Elder (*Tecoma stans*)

Yellow Shrimp Plant (*Pachystachys lutea*)

Perennials with Medium to High Salt Tolerance

Beach Sunflower (*Helianthus debilis*) High

Allamanda (*Allamanda cathartica*) Medium

Blackberry Lily (*Belamcanda chinensis*) Medium

Blanket Flower (*Gaillardia pulchella*) High

Blue Daze (*Evolvulus glomeratus*) Medium

Blue Sage (*Eranthemum pulchellum*) Medium

Bush Daisy (*Euryops pectinatus*) High

Chrysanthemum (*Chrysanthemum grandiflora*) Medium

Coneflower (*Echinacea purpurea*) Medium

Cuban Buttercup (*Turnera ulmifolia*) Medium

Cupflower (*Nierembergia caerulea*) Medium

Daylily (*Hemerocallis* hybrids) Medium

Dianthus (*Dianthus* species) Medium

Devil's Backbone (*Pedilanthus tithymaloides*) Medium

Firebush (*Hamelia patens*) Medium

Firecracker Plant (*Russelia equisetiformus*) Medium

Fleabane (*Erigeron karvinskianus* 'Profusion') Medium

Flowering Maple (*Abutilon hybridum*) Medium

Gerbera Daisy (*Gerbera jamesonii*) High

Golden Dewdrop (*Duranta repens*) Medium

Goldenrod (*Solidago* species) High

Heliconia (*Heliconia* species) Medium

Hibiscus (*Hibiscus grandiflorus*) High

Horsemint (*Monarda punctata*) Medium

Joseph's Coat (*Alternanthera* hybrids) Medium

Lantana (*Lantana* species) Medium

Lily of the Nile (*Agapanthus africanus*) Medium

Milkweed (*Asclepias tuberosa*) Medium

Mistflower (*Conoclinium coelestinum*) Medium

Persian Shield (*Strobilanthes dyerianus*) High

Porterweed (*Stachytarpheta* species) Medium

Sanchezia (*Sanchezia nobilis*) Medium

Society Garlic (*Tulbaghia fragrans*) Medium

Stonecrop (*Sedum* species) Medium

Tampa Verbain (*Glandularia tampensis*) Medium

Wormwood (*Artemisia* species) Medium

Yellow Elder (*Tecoma stans*) Medium

Perennials with Colorful Foliage

Begonia (*Begonia* hybrids)

Clerodendrum (*Clerodendrum quadriloculare* 'Variegata')

Creeping Jenny (*L. nummularia* 'Aurea')

Devil's Backbone (*Pedilanthus tithymaloides* 'Variegata')

Dragon's Breath (*Hemigraphis repanda*)

Elephant Ear (*Alocasia* species, *Xanthosoma* species, *Colocasia* hybrids)

Flax Lily (*Dianella tasmanica*)

Flowering Maple (*Abutilon pictum* 'Thompsonii,' *A.* 'Souvenir de Bonn')

Gingers (*Hedychium, Zingiber, Costus* species)

Golden Dewdrop (*Duranta repens* 'Aurea' and 'Variegata')

Hibiscus (*Hibiscus* 'Snow Queen')

Jewels of Opar (*Talinum paniculatum* 'Variegata' and 'Aurea')

Joseph's Coat (*Alternanthera* hybrids)

Key West Snow Bush (*Pseuderanthemum variegata*)

Leopard Plant (*Farfugium japonicum*)

Lily of the Nile (*Agapanthus africanus* 'Variegatus')

Louisiana Iris (*Iris japonica* 'Variegata')

Marble Leaf (*Peristrophe hyssopifolia* 'Aureo-variegata')

Ornamental Sweet Potato (*Ipomoea* hybrids)

Peacock Ginger (*Kaempferia, Cornukaempferia* 'Jungle Gold')

Persian Shield (*Strobilanthes dyerianus*)

Philippine Violet (*Barleria cristata* 'Variegata')

Plectranthus (*Plectranthus* species)

Polka Dot Plant (*Hypoestes phyllostachya*)

Red Dragon (*Persicaria microcephala*)

Red Flame Ivy (*Hemigraphis colorata*)

Sanchezia (*Sanchezia nobilis*)

Shrimp Plant (*Justicia brandegeana* 'Variegata')

Vinca major (*Vinca major* 'Variegata,' *Vinca major* 'maculata')

Whirling Butterflies (*Gaura lindheimeri*)

Wormwood (*Artemisia* 'Oriental Limelight')

Perennials with Fall into Winter Color in Florida Regions

Allamanda (*Allamanda cathartica*) South

Amethyst Star (*Pseuderanthemum laxiflorum*) Central, South

Angelonia (*Angelonia angustifolia*) South

Begonia (*Begonia* species) Central, South

Bird of Paradise (*Strelitzia reginae*) South

Blue Ginger (*Dichorisandra thyrsiflora*) Central, South

Blue Sage (*Eranthemum pulchellum*) Central, South

Butterfly Ginger (*Hedychium* species) Central, South

Chrysanthemum (*Chrysanthemum grandiflora*) All regions

Cigar Flower (*Cuphea ignea*) All regions

Clerodendrum (*Clerodendrum* species) South

Crossandra (*Crossandra infundibuliformis*) South

Cuban Buttercup (*Turnera ulmifolia*) South

Devil's Backbone (*Pedilanthus tithymaloides*) Central, South

Dianthus (*Dianthus* species) North, Central

Elephant Ear (*Colocasia* species) South

Firebush (*Hamelia patens*) Central, South

Firecracker (*Russelia equisetiformis*) Central, South

Firespike (*Odontonema cuspidata*) Central, South

Flowering Maple (*Abutilon hybridum*) Central, South

Ginger (*Costus* species, *Zingiber* species) Central, South

Golden Dewdrop (*Duranta repens*) Central, South

Golden plume (*Schaueria flavicoma*) South

Goldenrod (*Solidago* species) All regions

Gold Cestrum (*Cestrum aurantiacum*) All regions

Hemigraphis (*Hemigraphis colorata*) South

Hibiscus (*Hibiscus rosa-sinensis*) South

Hidden Ginger (*Curcuma* species) Central, South

Horsemint (*Monarda punctata*) All regions

Ironweed (*Vernonia gigantea*) All regions

Jacobinia (*Justicia carnea*) South

Jewels of Opar (*Talinum paniculatum* 'Aurea') South

Leopard Plant (*Farfugium japonicum*) All regions

Lion's Ear (*Leonotis leonurus*) All regions

Mistflower (*Conoclinium coelestinum*) All regions

Philippine Violet (*Barleria cristata*) All regions

Plectranthus (*Plectranthus* 'Mona Lavender') All regions

Plectranthus (*Plectranthus* species) All regions

Polka Dot Plant (*Hypoestes phyllostachya*) South

Porterweed (*Stachytarpheta* species) South

Rondeletia (*Rondeletia leucophylla*) Central, South

Ruellia (*Ruellia* species) South

Salvia (*Salvia* species) All regions

Sanchezia (*Sanchezia nobilis*) South

Sedum (*Sedum* species) All regions

Shrimp Plant (*Justicia brandegeana*) South

Swamp Sunflower (*Helianthus angustifolius*) All regions

Yellow Shrimp Plant (*Pachystachys lutea*) South

Perennials That Reseed

Aster (*Aster laevis*)

Beach Sunflower (*Helianthus debilis*)

Blackberry Lily (*Belamcanda chinensis*)

Black-eyed Susan (*Rudbeckia hirta*)

Blanket Flower (*Gaillardia pulchella*)

Brazilian Button Flower (*Centratherum punctatum*)

Cleome 'Linde Armstrong' (*Cleome* 'Linde Armstrong')

Clerodendrum (*Clerodendrum speciossimum*)

Coneflower (*Echinacea purpurea*)

Crossandra (*Crossandra infundibuliformis*)

Cuban Buttercup (*Turnera ulmifolia*)

Fleabane (*Erigeron karvinskianus* 'Profusion')

Goldenrod (*Solidago* species)

Horsemint (*Monarda punctata*)

Ironweed (*Vernonia gigantea*)

Lantana (*Lantana* species)

Milkweed (*Asclepias* species)

Mistflower (*Conoclinium coelestinum*)

Peacock Ginger (*Kaempferia* species)

Phillipine Violet (*Barleria cristata*)

Polka Dot Plant (*Hypoestes phyllostachya*)

Porterweed (*Stachytarpheta* species)

Ruellia (*Ruellia* species)

Salvia (*Salvia coccinea*)

Scorpion's Tail (*Heliotropium angiospermum*)

Swamp Sunflower (*Helianthus angustifolius*)

Tampa Verbain (*Glandularia tampensis*)

Verbena (*Verbena bonariensis*)

Native Perennials

Aster (*Aster carolinianus*)

Beach Sunflower (*Helianthus debilis*)

Black-eyed Susan (*Rudbeckia hirta, R. triloba*)

Blanket Flower (*Gaillardia pulchella*)

Coneflower (*Echinacea purpurea*)

Firebush (*Hamelia patens*)

Goldenrod (*Solidago sempervirens, S. odora*)

Hibiscus (*Hibiscus coccineus, H. moscheutos*)

Horsemint (*Monarda punctata*)

Iris (*Iris hexagonae*)

Ironweed (*Vernonia gigantea*)

Lantana (*Lantana depressa, L. involucrata*)

Milkweed (*Asclepias perennis, A. tuberose*)

Mistflower (*Conoclinium coelestinum*)

Phlox (*Phlox divaricata*)

Plumbago (*Plumbago scandens*)

Porterweed (*Stachytarpheta jamaicensis*)

Ruellia (*Ruellia caroliniensis*)

Saltmarsh Mallow (*Kosteletzkya virginica*)

Salvia (*Salvia lyrata, S. coccinea*)

Scorpion-tail (*Heliotropium angiospermum*)

Skullcap (some *Scutellaria* species)

Stokes Aster (*Stokesia laevis*)

Swamp Sunflower (*Helianthus angustfolius*)

Tampa Verbain (*Glandularia tampensis*)

Verbena (some *Verbena* species)

Perennials with Fragrant Flowers or Foliage

Angelonia (*Angelonia angustifolia*)

Chrysanthemum (*Chrysanthemum grandiflora*)

Clerodendrum (some *Clerodendrum* species)

Coneflower (*Echinacea purpurea*)

Dianthus (*Dianthus* species)

Ginger (*Hedychium* species, *Costus speciosa* 'Alba')

Louisiana Iris (*Iris* species)

Night Blooming Jasmine (*Cestrum nocturnum*)

Plectranthus (*Plectranthus* species)

Salvia (*Salvia officianalis, S. fruticosa, S. elegans*)

Society Garlic (*Tulbaghia fragrans*)

Wormwood (*Artemisia* species)

Perennials for Cut Flowers

Angelonia (*Angelonia angustifolia*)

Aster (*Aster laevis*)

Bird of Paradise (*Strelitzia reginae*)

Black-eyed Susan (*Rudbeckia* species)

Blanket Flower (*Gaillardia pulchella*)

Brazilian Snapdragon (*Otacanthus azureus*)

Cat's Whiskers (*Orthosiphon stamineus*)

Chrysanthemum (*Chrysanthemum grandiflora*)

Cleome 'Linda Armstrong' (*Cleome* 'Linda Armstrong')

Clerodendrum (*Clerodendrum* species)

Coneflower (*Echinacea purpurea*)

Dianthus (*Dianthus caryophyllus*)

False Dragon Head (*Physostegia virginiana*)

Firespike (*Odontonema cuspidata*)

Fleabane (*Erigeron karvinskianus* 'Profusion')

Gerbera Daisy (*Gerbera jamesonii*)

Gingers (*Curcuma, Heliconia, Alpinia, Zingiber* species)

Golden Plume (*Schaueria flavicoma*)

Goldenrod (*Solidago* species)

Heliconia (*Heliconia* species)

Horsemint (*Monarda punctata*)

Hosta (*Hosta* species)

Ironweed (*Vernonia gigantea*)

Jacobinia (*Justicia carnea*)

Lily of the Nile (*Agapanthus* hybrids)

Lion's Ear (*Leonotis leonurus*)

Louisiana Iris (*Iris* species)

Mistflower (*Conoclinium coelestinum*)

Obedient Plant (*Physostegia virginiana*)

Pentas (*Pentas lanceolata*)

Phlox (*Phlox divaricata*)

Plumbago (*Plumbago auriculata, P. scandens*)

Rondeletia (*Rondeletia leucophylla*)

Ruellia (*Ruellia caroliniensis*)

Salvia (*Salvia* species)

Shasta Daisy (*Leucanthemum superbum*)

Shrimp Plant (*Justicia brandegeana*)

Stokes Aster (*Stokesia laevis*)

Swamp Sunflower (*Helianthus angustifolius*)

Verbena (*Verbena* species)

Yarrow (*Achillea* species)

Yellow Shrimp Plant (*Pachystachys lutea*)

Perennials That Attract Butterflies

Aster (*Aster laevis*)

Beach Sunflower (*Helianthus debilis*)

Black-eyed Susan (*Rudbeckia* species)

Blanket Flower (*Gaillardia pulchella*)

Brazilian Button Flower (*Centratherum punctatum*)

Bush Daisy (*Euryops pectinatus*)

Cat's Whiskers (*Orthosiphon stamineus*)

Chrysanthemum (*Chrysanthemum grandiflora*)

Cigar Flower (*Cuphea ignea*)

Clerodendrum (*Clerodendrum* species)

Coneflower (*Echinacea purpurea*)

Firebush (*Hamelia patens*)

Firecracker Plant (*Russelia species*)

Firespike (*Odontonema cuspidata*)

Flowering Maple (*Abutilon hybridum*)

Gerbera Daisy (*Gerbera jamesonii*)

Gingers (*Hedychium* species)

Golden Dewdrop (*Duranta repens*)

Golden plume (*Schaueria flavicoma*)

Goldenrod (*Solidago* species)

Heliotrope (*Heliotropium angiospermum*)

Hibiscus (*Hibiscus rosa-sinensis*)

Horsemint (*Monarda punctata*)

Ironweed (*Vernonia gigantea*)

Lantana (*Lantana* species)

Lion's Ear (*Leonotis leonurus*)

Mexican Heather (*Cuphea hyssopifolia*)

Milkweed (*Asclepias* species)

Mistflower (*Conoclinium coelestinum*)

Pentas (*Pentas lanceolata*)

Phlox (*Phlox* species)

Plumbago (*Plumbago auriculata*)

Porterweed (*Stachytarpheta* species)

Rondeletia (*Rondeletia leucophylla*)

Ruellia (*Ruellia* species)

Salvia (*Salvia* species)

Sedum (*Sedum* species)

Shrimp Plant (*Justicia brandegeana*)

Skull Cap (*Scutellaria* species)

Stokes Aster (*Stokesia laevis*)

Swamp Sunflower (*Helianthus angustifolius*)

Tampa Verbain (*Glandularia tampensis*)

Verbena (*Verbena* hybrids)

Yarrow (*Achillea* species)

Yellow Shrimp Plant (*Pachystachys lutea*)

Perennials That Attract Hummingbirds

Cat's Whiskers (*Orthosiphon stamineus*)

Cleome 'Linde Armstrong' (*Cleome* 'Linde Armstrong')

Clerodendrum (*Clerodendrum* species)

Firebush (*Hamelia patens*)

Firecracker (*Russelia equisetiformis*)

Firespike (*Odontonema cuspidata*)

Flowering Maple (*Abutilon hybridum*)

Gingers (*Hedychium* and *Costus* species)

Golden Dewdrop (*Duranta repens*)

Hibiscus (*Hibiscus* species)

Horsemint (*Monarda punctata*)

Lantana (*Lantana* species)

Pentas (*Pentas lanceolata*)

Plumbago (*Plumbago auriculata*)

Porterweed (*Stachytarpheta* species)

Salvia (*Salvia* species)

Shrimp Plant (*Justicia brandegeana*)

Perennials That May Be Invasive in Your Area of the State

Clerodendrum (*Clerodendrum* species)

Cuban Buttercup (*Turnera ulmifolia*)

Elephant Ear (*Colocasia* species)

Firecracker (*Russelia equisetiformis*)

Golden Dewdrop (*Duranta repens*)

Jewels of Opar (*Talinum paniculatum*)

Joseph's Coat (*Alternanthera* species)

Lantana (*Lantana camara*)

Philippine Violet (*Barleria cristata*)

This mixture of perennials provides color, texture, and a feeling of lush greenery year round.

four

Planting and Establishing Perennials ✦

The first step in the planting process is to water the plant well *before* it goes in the ground. Never plant a dry or wilted plant. Irrigating for an hour after planting will not replace a good soaking before planting.

Next, gently remove the plant from its container and examine the root ball. If the plant is very rootbound, consider gently loosening the roots. However, there is no real proof that this is beneficial, and some fragile rooted perennials can actually be damaged.

The planting hole you dig should be twice as wide, and no deeper, than the root ball of the plant. Loosening and aerating the soil in this way will help ensure that the plant roots get the oxygen they need to establish, survive, and grow. Research has shown that adding amendments (such as peat or compost) just to the planting hole does not benefit the plant. The roots soon outgrow the amended area. However, as mentioned previously, adding organic amendments to the *entire* bed is very beneficial.

The plant should be placed in the planting hole so that the top of the root ball is even with the soil surface. Fill the hole completely, making sure that no soil is placed on top of the root ball. Gently press the soil in around the root ball, but do not forcefully compact the soil with your hand or foot. Water well. The main goal in correct planting is to match the top of the root ball with the surrounding soil level. A root ball that is buried too deeply or protrudes from the soil is subject to stress and disease.

Once you have planted and watered your perennials it is time to mulch. Apply mulch 2–3 inches deep between plants, but less deep (¼-inch layer) at the base of each plant. Too much mulch piled up against the stems of your flowers encourages stem rot.

Presently in Florida, the most common mulches are ground-up trees (cypress, melaleuca, eucalyptus), pine straw, and shredded or chipped pine bark. You can also use leaves that have fallen in your yard, newspapers, or grass clippings. Some counties sell or give away mulch recycled from yard waste. In general, wood mulches tend to last longer in the garden than others, but all mulches need to be replenished at least once a year. {Photo 4.05 near here}

Mulching provides a variety of benefits for the perennial garden:

1 Mulch defines and beautifies plant beds.

2 Mulch acts as a blanket that holds water in the soil. You won't need to water as often and your plants benefit from the consistent moisture.

3 Mulch moderates soil temperature. It insulates roots from the heat of summer and the cold of winter.

4 Mulch reduces disease problems by preventing rain and irrigation from splashing soil and disease pathogens onto lower leaves and flowers.

5 Finally, a thick layer of mulch will inhibit weeds from ruining your efforts. Weed seeds need sunlight to germinate and a thick mulch serves to block light from the soil surface.

Frequent watering is essential to establish newly planted perennials. Frequency depends on time of year, soil type, and light (sun or shade). Water daily for the first three days and then taper off gradually. Most perennials require two to three months to become well established. Once established, perennials should be watered "as needed." A regular deep watering is always best. Again, the site and season will determine the frequency, but the amount should be consistent ($\frac{1}{2}$–$\frac{3}{4}$ inches per application). This will wet a sandy soil 6–10 inches deep—the normal root depth of most perennials.

Make sure you water plants well before planting.

Healthy perennials should have a vigorous root system.

Planting hole should be wider than the root ball but no deeper.

Apply an even layer of mulch around each plant.

Mulching provides many benefits.

*Different forms and colors of Plectranthus
make a beautiful combination.*

five

Maintaining Your Perennial Garden

Maintaining a perennial garden is much easier with proper bed preparation, plant selection, planting, and mulching. Remember, like all plants, perennials have certain cultural needs that must be met.

Fertilizing

The Florida-friendly approach to fertilizing encourages the use of products that contain slow release nutrients. Apply these forms of fertilizer on an "as-needed" basis. In other words, assess the nutritional needs of your plants based on the season, amount of rainfall and irrigation, growth rate, and plant appearance. Remember, too much fertilizer can lead to problems—not only for the environment, but also for your garden. High levels of fertilizer (particularly nitrogen) can reduce winter and root hardiness, encourage disease and insect problems, and promote over-growth.

Most garden soils in Florida already contain adequate phosphorus for perennials, so look for fertilizer formulations with a low middle number (e.g., 18-6-12, 15-4-15). Too much phosphorus can cause nutritional imbalances in plants. When plants are grown in containers using potting mixes, a fertilizer containing higher phosphorus levels is appropriate. Follow label instructions for the amount to apply.

You can apply fertilizer in several ways. One is to broadcast or spread the fertilizer over the entire bed. Make sure to wash granular or controlled-release fertilizers off the foliage to avoid burning the leaves.

Succeeding with perennials requires regular maintenance. Frequent watering is essential to establishing new plants.

Or: Apply the fertilizer just around the base of individual plants. This is a bit more work but is probably more efficient when plants are small. Keep fertilizer at least 2–3 inches away from the base to avoid burning the stems. Or apply liquid fertilizers. Water-soluble fertilizer is readily absorbed by plants, and is the best way to quickly correct nutrient deficiencies. However, soluble fertilizers leach or move through soils quickly and must be applied frequently.

Pruning

Like most plants, perennials need occasional pruning. Shaping of plants is done whenever plants outgrow their area or become straggly. Deadheading is a pruning technique where only old flowers and seed heads are removed. This is done for aesthetic reasons and/or to encourage new flowers.

Finally, some perennials require annual pruning to remove dead or damaged foliage. Certain perennials naturally die back to the ground during winter and dead tissue can be removed immediately. However, when plants are killed back by frosts or freezes, pruning should be postponed until spring growth commences and the extent of injury can be assessed.

Deadheading (removing spent flowers) encourages new flowers.

Weed Control

Weeds are the biggest nuisance in the perennial garden; their management can be accomplished in several ways. Mulching, as mentioned, will go far in preventing many annual weeds. Hand-pulling weed seedlings as soon as they appear or before they go to seed will keep weeds from reseeding in the garden. Chemical herbicides are another option. Weeds can be prevented using pre-emergent herbicides that kill weed seeds as they sprout. Apply the chemical around plants according to label directions. Do not use pre-emergent weed killers in beds where flower seeds will be planted or where you want certain plants to reseed themselves.

Post-emergent herbicides control weeds *after* they germinate and begin growing. This type of chemical weed control must be done very carefully as most post-emergent weed killers cannot distinguish between a weed and a desirable perennial. Use care in selecting the weed killers you use in the garden as they can be very specific about which weeds they control. The IFAS publication *Weeds of Southern Turfgrass* is an excellent resource for weed identification.

Watering

The best way to water any flowerbed is with a "micro-irrigation" system. Micro-irrigation (drip emitters, drip tubing, or micro-sprayers) efficiently applies water directly to the soil where roots can absorb it. Many off-the-shelf kits can be connected to a garden hose or spigot. Or you may want to consider retrofitting existing in-ground sprinklers with micro-irrigation devices. When installed and operated correctly, these systems save water, money, and time. The least desirable way to water perennials is overhead irrigation, which can encourage diseases and damage flowers.

Micro-irrigation systems are efficient and exempt from water restrictions in some areas of the state.

Insects and Diseases

The perennials listed in this book are, for the most part, easy to grow and fairly pest free. Keep in mind that many insects and diseases are "opportunistic," meaning they take advantage of plants already under stress. For example, planting a sun-loving perennial in too much shade and then overwatering will result in fungal diseases of the leaves and roots. Honoring the golden rule of gardening—"Right Plant/Right Place"—will always pay off in healthier, more pest-resistant plants.

However, an insect or disease occasionally will emerge because of inclement weather or some other fluke of Mother Nature. Most diseases you encounter in the perennial garden will be fungal diseases because they thrive in Florida's warm, wet weather. When a disease is suspected, pick or prune off infected plant parts and spray with a fungicide to protect unaffected growth.

Most insects and mites are suppressed by naturally occurring beneficial parasites, predators, and diseases. However, you may need to intercede occasionally, when it appears that the "good guys" are losing the battle. Using pesticides only as needed will protect the many beneficial insects, butterflies, and hummingbirds that a flower garden attracts and sustains. Contact your county's Extension office for advice on the safest and most effective pesticides to use. See the bibliography for information on how to contact your county's Extension office.

Cold Protection

Cold protection can be an important issue if you are growing tropical perennials. The best form of cold protection is a thick layer of mulch. The mulch acts as a blanket to keep the soil and plant roots warm. Most tropical perennials resprout from their roots and recover quickly from cold injury.

Tropical perennials may occasionally need cold protection. Make sure covers reach to the ground.

Covering plants during frosts and freezes in Florida will also help protect your plants. Covers trap heat rising from the soil and will keep plants a few degrees warmer than the outside temperature. The cover must extend all the way to the ground. Blankets, tarps, plastic, or frost cloth will help in mild frosts or freezes but do not prevent damage in the event of a hard freeze. Gardeners need to choose for themselves which plants they will use in their garden. It is always most sensible (and less work) to select plants that naturally tolerate the cold in your region.

So get going! Use this guide to Florida perennials and the other resources listed to transform your yard into the garden you have always wanted.

Bibliography

Black, R. J. *Salt Tolerant Plants for Florida.* Fact Sheet ENH-26. Gainesville: Environmental Horticulture Department, Florida Cooperative
Extension Service, Institute of Food and Agricultural Sciences,
University of Florida. First published: Dec 1985. <http://edis.ifas.
ufl.edu/ EP012>, accessed February 2005.

Griffiths, Mark. *Index of Garden Plants.* Portland, Ore.: Timber Press,
1994.

Haynes, Jody, John McLaughlin, Laura Vasquez, and Adrian Hunsberger.
Low Maintenance Landscape Plants for South Florida. Fact Sheet ENH-
854. Gainesville: Environmental Horticulture Department, Florida
Cooperative Extension Service, Institute of Food and Agricultural
Sciences, University of Florida. First published: Dec 2001. *<http://
edis.ifas.ufl.edu/ep107>,* accessed June 2005.

Nelson, Gil. *Florida's Best Native Landscape Plants: 200 Readily Available
Species for Homeowners and Professionals.* Gainesville: University Press
of Florida, 2003.

Osorio, Rufino. *A Gardener's Guide to Florida's Native Plants.* Gainesville:
University Press of Florida, 2001.

Park Brown, Sydney, Loretta Hodyss, and David Marshall. *Flowering
Perennials for Florida.* Fact Sheet ENH-68. Gainesville: Environmental
Horticulture Department, Florida Cooperative Extension Service,
Institute of Food and Agricultural Sciences, University of Florida. First
published: May 1991. Revised: June 1996. <http://edis.ifas.ufl.edu/
mg035>, accessed January 2005.

Tjia, B., and S. A. Rose. "Salt Tolerant Bedding Plants." *Proceedings of the
Florida Horticulture Society* 100: 181–182, 1987.

Watkins, John V., and Herbert S. Wolfe. *Your Florida Garden,* 5th ed.
Gainesville: University Press of Florida, 1974.

Wunderlin, R. P., and B. F. Hansen. "Atlas of Florida Vascular Plants."
Institute for Systematic Botany, University of South Florida, Tampa.
<http://www.plantatlas.usf.edu>, accessed June 2004.

The following Web site lists the Cooperative Extension offices in each
county in Florida. Use this link to contact your local county Extension
office. <http://www.ifas.ufl.edu/extension/cesmap.htm>.

Index

Sydney Park Brown is an Extension horticulture agent with the University of Florida/IFAS Extension Service with more than twenty-nine years of experience. She recently joined the University of Florida's teaching program as an adjunct faculty member at the Plant City campus.

Rick K. Schoellhorn is director of new products for Proven Winners, an international plant branding and marketing company. He was formerly with the University of Florida where he was an Extension floriculture specialist and associate professor in the Department of Environmental Horticulture.

Related-interest titles from University Press of Florida

Citrus Growing in Florida, Fourth Edition
Larry K. Jackson and Frederick S. Davies

Florida Butterfly Caterpillars and Their Host Plants
Marc C. Minno, Jerry F. Butler, and Donald W. Hall

Florida Landscape Plants: Native and Exotic, Second Revised Edition
John V. Watkins, Thomas J. Sheehan, and Robert J. Black

The Florida Lawn Handbook: Best Management Practices for Your Home Lawn in Florida, Third Edition
Laurie E. Trenholm and J. Bryan Unruh

Florida Wildflowers in Their Natural Communities
Walter Kingsley Taylor

Landscape Plants for the Gulf and South Atlantic Coasts: Selection, Establishment, and Maintenance
Robert J. Black and Edward F. Gilman

Palms of South Florida
George B. Stevenson

Vegetable Gardening in Florida
James M. Stephens

Wild Orchids of Florida, Updated and Expanded Edition with References to the Atlantic and Gulf Coastal Plains
Paul Martin Brown with drawings by Stan Folsom

Your Florida Garden
John V. Watkins and Herbert S. Wolfe

Your Florida Guide to Bedding Plants: Selection, Establishment, and Maintenance
Robert J. Black and Edward F. Gilman

Your Florida Guide to Shrubs: Selection, Establishment, and Maintenance
Edward F. Gilman and Robert J. Black

Your Florida Landscape: A Complete Guide to Planting and Maintenance
Robert J. Black and Kathleen Ruppert

For more information on these and other books, visit our website at www.upf.com.